FROM THE AUTHOR

The words in this book flow from a conviction that God intends for your faith to intersect with your everyday life.

Many people hang out with God for an hour on Sunday and then ignore him for the rest of the week. Or they have a ten-minute "quiet time" in the morning, and then leave God behind and get on with the business of the real world. But the real world is the only place in which you can live out your faith in God. He wants you to pay attention to him not only while you sing on Sunday, but all week long while you wash dishes or negotiate contracts or take algebra tests or sit in traffic or whatever else you do. He wants to go with you to the office, the classroom, the coffee shop, the soccer field, and every other stop on your route each day. Both your faith and your everyday life will be enriched when they experience more regular contact with each other. My hope is that these devotions will help to facilitate that contact.

This book is yours now, and you can use it however you desire. But I would suggest that you read one of the readings each weekday, in the middle of the day, in the middle of your normal activities. Let it be a divine interruption that helps you to pay attention to him right in the midst of the real world. Let it refresh you and remind you that God is God and he is with you and he can make an impact on the way you live the rest of your day.

May God use this book to make you more impressed with him, and more willing to let him work in you and through you each day.

Blake McKinney is the husband of Gayla, the father of Justin, Caleb, and Sarah, and the pastor of First Baptist Church of Lee's Summit, Missouri. He loves helping people live out their faith in God in their everyday lives.

To Gayla, Justin, Caleb, and Sarah

Being connected to the four of you is the best part of being me!

ACKNOWLEDGEMENTS

I'm grateful to those of you who have subscribed to the daily email devotions I have written throughout the last few years. Hearing you talk about times that a certain devotion seemed to be written just for you at just the right time has encouraged me to continue to write. Thanks to those of you at Lost Mountain Baptist Church and First Baptist Church of Lee's Summit—you have been the primary audience and guinea pigs for these words, and your feedback has been invaluable. And much gratitude to Jeremy Lokey, Eddie Parker, and Carl Gregg—without your computer skills, nobody would have read a one of these things.

I'm especially thankful to J.V. McKinney, my father and the best photographer I know, for sharing some of his awesome pictures. Dad, your photos are more "refreshing" than a thousand of my words, and I love the way they confirm the truths presented in the devotions.

CONTENTS

Week 1: With Us	1
Week 2: Mercy	7
Week 3: Listen	13
Week 4: Mouth and Mind	19
Week 5: Transformation	25
Week 6: Satisfaction	31
Week 7: Risk	37
Week 8: Savoring Scripture	43
Week 9: Conflict	49
Week 10: God Is Strong	55
Week 11: Worry	61
Week 12: Worry	67
Week 13: Name Trashing	73
Week 14: God Forgets	79
Week 15: Temptation	85
Week 16: Temptation	91
Week 17: Relief	97
Week 18: Love	103
Week 19: Love	109
Week 20: Numbered Days	115
Week 21: Courage	121
Week 22: Courage	127
Week 23: God's Will	133
Week 24: Complaining	139

Week 25: Solitude   145

Week 26: Judging   151

Week 27: Lord's Prayer   157

Week 28: Lord's Prayer   163

Week 29: Patience   169

Week 30: Audience of One   175

Week 31: Slow Down   181

Week 32: God Metaphors   187

Week 33: Work   193

Week 34: Adopted   199

Week 35: Self Control   205

Week 36: God the Giver   211

Week 37: God the Giver   217

Week 38: Mouth Filter   223

Week 39: Doubt   229

Week 40: Perseverance   235

Week 41: Anxiety   241

Week 42: Incomparable Christ   247

Week 43: Servanthood   253

Week 44: Thought Life   259

Week 45: Peace   265

Week 46: Peace   271

Week 47: Heaven   277

Week 48: God's Questions   283

Week 49: Confession   289

Week 50: Impact   295

Week 51: Double Minded   301

Week 52: Today   307

WEEK 1: WITH US

DAY 1

LISTEN TO THE WORD

Where can I go from your Spirit?
Where can I flee from your presence?
(Psalm 139:7)

In Psalm 139, the psalm writer celebrates that the answer to the questions in verse 7 is "absolutely nowhere." No matter where today takes you, God will be there. You can't shake him by traveling a great distance. Your mistakes won't make him give up and go away. His presence overflows every square inch of our vast universe. He will be there when you have to make the day's most important decision. He will be there when you experience the high point of your day. He will be there when things get tough. He will be there in the countless mundane moments in between. God is always with you.

LIVE THE WORD

Try a little experiment today: wherever you go, picture Jesus with you. Imagine him sitting in the nearby chair, riding in the passenger seat, or walking beside you. Interact with him as if he were right there with you — because he is!

Day 2

Listen to the Word

Have I not commanded you? Be strong and courageous.
Do not be afraid; do not be discouraged, for the Lord your God
will be with you wherever you go.
(Joshua 1:9)

God commanded Joshua, and us, not to be afraid. That sounds like an impossible instruction to follow. Like you, Joshua had plenty of reasons to be terrified. He was stepping into the un-fillable shoes of Moses; he was being enlisted to lead a bunch of cantankerous ex-slaves who didn't want to follow; he was about to wage war against battle-tested troops in fortified cities. He had reasons for fear. So do you. You deal with family struggles, financial struggles, health struggles — you have a thousand reasons to be afraid. But you have one reason to be strong and courageous: "The Lord your God will be with you wherever you go." That is reason enough.

Live the Word

What are you facing that is most likely to leave you terrified or discouraged? In prayer, ask God to handle that challenge. Ask him to remind you that he is bigger than what you fear.

DAY 3

LISTEN TO THE WORD

…Surely I am with you always, to the very end of the age.
(Matthew 28:20)

The book of Matthew ends with a remarkable promise from Jesus: he will always be with you. If you have given your life to him, you will never be alone. Every time you enjoy a victory, he is right there to celebrate with you. Every time you struggle, he is there to help. When you fall, he reaches out to pull you back onto your feet. As a follower of Jesus, you are not just living your life for him; you get to live life with him. He is with you always. He is with you right now.

LIVE THE WORD

Take a moment to tell Jesus "thanks" for his promise to be with you all the time. Ask him to help you be aware that he is with you throughout this day and this week.

DAY 4

LISTEN TO THE WORD

And whatever you do, whether in word or deed, do it all in the name
of the Lord Jesus, giving thanks to God the Father through him.
(Colossians 3:17)

We tend to separate our lives into compartments of "sacred" and
"secular." We would say that praying is sacred, but mowing the grass is
secular. Reading the Bible is sacred, but reading a chemistry textbook is
secular. Colossians 3:17 obliterates that distinction. It tells us that every
moment can be sacred time. "Whatever you do" can be done in Jesus'
name. Even the most ordinary, mundane task can become something you
do for Christ's sake. Your daily work can become an act of worship. Your
daily tasks can be done in partnership with him.

LIVE THE WORD

What is your next task for the day? Make an effort to do that task "in
the name of the Lord Jesus." Do it as he would do it if he were in your
place. Do it for him, and realize that he is with you as you go.

WEEK 1: WITH US

DAY 5

LISTEN TO THE WORD

Even though I walk through the darkest valley,
I will fear no evil, for you are with me....
(Psalm 23:4)

You may be in the middle of a dark valley right now. If you are not, you can be sure one is waiting for you down the road somewhere. Psalm 23:4 offers two bits of great news for us when we are in the valley. First, the darkness is temporary. It says we walk "through" the valley. We can look forward to coming out on the other side. Second, we do not walk alone! Even in the gloomy times, God is with us. Like a small child has the courage to enter a dark room when Mom or Dad goes with her, we can draw strength from the knowledge that our Creator accompanies us through the dark valleys of our lives. Fear is pointless, because God is with us!

LIVE THE WORD

Every time you feel fear or dread creeping into your mind today, shoo it away by reminding yourself that you are not alone. Your Father, whose strength has no limits, is with you.

Week 2: Mercy

WEEK 2: MERCY

DAY 1

LISTEN TO THE WORD

Who is a God like you, who pardons sin and forgives
the transgression of the remnant of his inheritance? You do not
stay angry forever but delight to show mercy.
(Micah 7:18)

Perhaps the most surprising characteristic of God is his mercy. We would expect God to be holy and powerful and wise and impressive in lots of other ways. But merciful? You wouldn't guess that a flawless God would extend grace to flawed folks like us. You wouldn't imagine that a God who has never made a mistake would be patient with the loads of mistakes that we make. Yet Micah tells us that God delights to show mercy. It makes him smile to give you blessings you don't deserve, to forgive your flaws, and to give you second chances.

We will spend the week reflecting on the mercy of God. Be ready to be captured by his amazing grace!

LIVE THE WORD

Ask God to astonish you this week with the depth of his mercy. Pray that he will strip away any illusion that you may have that he loves you because of how good you are, or that he doesn't love you because of how bad you are.

DAY 2

LISTEN TO THE WORD

The Lord our God is merciful and forgiving,
even though we have rebelled against him.
(Daniel 9:9)

We normally love something because there is something about that thing that causes us to love it. I love French fries because they taste good. A boy loves his girlfriend because she is cute, or funny, or smart, or kind. We love things that deserve to be loved — things that have inherent worth.

God's love for us is different. He does not love us because of something in us. He loves us because of something in him. God loves us not because *we* are good, but because *he* is good. As Daniel observed, he shows us mercy even though we have rebelled against him. No matter how unlovable we may be, God loves us anyway. That's just the way he is!

LIVE THE WORD

Think of something you have done that would have shut you off from God if his love were based on how much you deserve it. Thank him for loving you in spite of everything. Thank him for his mercy.

DAY 3

LISTEN TO THE WORD

Have mercy on me, Lord, for I call to you all day long. (Psalm 86:3)

You might expect that God would only pay attention to the prayers of people who are especially holy. Perhaps we assume that if we want God to hear our prayers, we should polish up our religious résumés. We might pray, "Lord, I have been to church for several weeks in a row. I have been reading my Bible a little more. I've mostly been nice to people. I have even tried to floss my teeth more lately. Since I've been so good, please answer my prayer."

But the psalmist realizes that the foundation of prayer is God's mercy, not our merit. God is not waiting for you to "measure up" before he will hear your prayers. Don't bother with trying to impress him. He wants you to come to him just as you are.

LIVE THE WORD

As you pray today, be aware of the fact that your ability to come into God's presence is not something you have achieved as a reward for good behavior—it is a gift of God's mercy.

DAY 4

LISTEN TO THE WORD

As Jesus went on from there, two blind men followed him,
calling out, "Have mercy on us, Son of David!"
(Matthew 9:27)

The blind men in Matthew 9 were among many who called for
mercy from Jesus. And countless people received mercy from him. There
were prostitutes — women who had taken their God-designed bodies,
God's temples, and used them shamefully. Jesus forgave them. There
were lepers — outcasts suffering from a disease that left them unclean
in every possible way. Jesus healed them. There were tax collectors —
greedy turncoats getting rich off their neighbors. Jesus dined with them
and called them as his disciples. There were friends who denied him,
pretending they had never met him. Jesus gave them second chances.
Jesus is full of mercy.

LIVE THE WORD

Experiment with a "breath prayer" today. Repeat the simple plea,
"Lord, have mercy," multiple times throughout the day.

DAY 5

LISTEN TO THE WORD

Be merciful, just as your Father is merciful. (Luke 6:36)

In Luke 6, Jesus challenges you to take the mercy you have received from God and extend it to the people in your life. Just as mercy marks the character of God, it must mark yours. There ought to be a family resemblance between the Father and his child. The God who forgives freely and loves lavishly calls you to do the same. If God has mercifully pardoned your faults, why should you refuse to pardon the offenses of others? You can show your appreciation for the countless second chances God has given you by extending second chances to those who disappoint you.

LIVE THE WORD

Are you holding onto a grudge against someone? Ask God to help you let it go and extend his mercy to that person. Ask God to help you be more like him.

WEEK 3: LISTEN

WEEK 3: LISTEN

DAY 1

LISTEN TO THE WORD

…Speak, for your servant is listening. (1 Samuel 3:10)

The Bible is the story of a God who likes to talk. According to Genesis, he *spoke* the universe into existence. He entered the world as Jesus, the *Word* made flesh. The pages of Scripture are filled with stories of God speaking to all kinds of people. He spoke to spiritual giants and leaders, but he also spoke to regular folks and rejects and rebels. He spoke to small children and to people who had been AARP-eligible for decades.

God still speaks today. He did not go mute after the final page of Scripture was written. He has not developed laryngitis. If you have a relationship with him, you can expect him to speak to you — that's what people in relationships do. God has something to say to you! Are you ready to listen?

LIVE THE WORD

Tell God "thanks" for being a God who speaks. Make Samuel's prayer yours, and repeat it often this week: "Speak, Lord, for your servant is listening!"

DAY 2

LISTEN TO THE WORD

When Jesus had finished saying these things, the crowds were amazed at
his teaching, because he taught as one who had authority....
(Matthew 7:28–29)

How can we recognize God's voice? We want him to speak to us. But
how can we know that what we hear is coming from him? Dallas Willard
observed that God's voice has some distinguishing marks. The first mark
is its quality: God speaks with authority. In Matthew 7, we read that what
blew people away about Jesus' teaching was that he spoke with authority.
God does not have to argue or try to convince; he simply speaks, and his
words have an unmistakable weight and impact that incline us to obey.
The second mark of God's voice is its spirit: God speaks with a spirit
of love, peace, and joy. The third mark of God's voice is its content: his
words are always consistent with Biblical truth and the example of Jesus.[1]

Just as it is with human voices, the more time you spend in conversation with God, the more natural it will become to recognize his voice.

LIVE THE WORD

The next time you open your Bible, read the words as a personal
letter from God to you. Ask him to speak to you through what you read.

---

[1] Dallas Willard, *Hearing God* (Downers Grove, Ill.: InterVarsity, 1999), pp. 174-178.

DAY 3

LISTEN TO THE WORD

If anyone has ears to hear, let them hear. (Mark 4:23)

Jesus recognized that having two ears attached to our heads does not necessarily make us listeners. Often our attitudes serve to filter out God's voice. For example, you won't have ears to hear God if you desire to continue running your own life. If you ask God to give you his opinion about something, but you reserve the right to ignore that advice if you don't like it, you won't be in much of a position to hear. You also won't have ears to hear God if you only listen for him when you are in trouble or are facing a tough decision. Aren't you frustrated by a "friend" who only calls when they need you to bail them out of trouble? You will be much more likely to hear God's voice in the crisis times when you are in the habit of listening to him day by day.

LIVE THE WORD

Be honest with God. Confess to him your tendency toward selective listening. Ask God to shape you into a person who consistently listens to and obeys his voice.

DAY 4

LISTEN TO THE WORD

The Lord will guide you always.... (Isaiah 58:11)

What an amazing promise: your Heavenly Father assures you that he will give you constant guidance and direction. He loves you so much that he has made a plan for this day of your life. He knows you inside and out; he knows all about your needs and the needs around you; he sees all the challenges you see, and sees them more accurately than you do, and he even sees the ones that are looming over the horizon beyond your view. He took all of that into account, and he formed the best possible plan for you. Now, he wants to let you in on his plan. He wants to guide you — today and always.

LIVE THE WORD

Today, pay a special kind of attention to what you read, what your friends say, and what is going on in your circumstances and in your heart. Listen for God's voice. Ask God to use those tools and any other means he chooses to speak to you and guide you.

DAY 5

LISTEN TO THE WORD

I no longer call you servants, because a servant does not know his
master's business. Instead, I have called you friends, for everything that
I learned from my Father I have made known to you.
(John 15:15)

Jesus said that if you were nothing more than his servant, you
wouldn't expect him to speak to you. But you are more than a servant.
Jesus calls you his friend! Because you are his friend, he wants to tell you
his business. He wants you to be "in the loop" regarding his plans to work
in you and around you. He wants to speak to you, and he wants you to
listen. And we are talking about more than an occasional nudge or case of
spiritual goosebumps. He wants you to enjoy a conversational relationship
with him. He wants to talk with you, friend to friend.

LIVE THE WORD

Be silent for a moment. Don't say anything to God. Simply listen for
him to speak to you.

Week 4: Mouth and Mind

WEEK 4: MOUTH AND MIND

DAY 1

LISTEN TO THE WORD

May these words of my mouth and this meditation of my heart be
pleasing in your sight, LORD, my Rock and my Redeemer.
(Psalm 19:14)

Psalm 19:14 announces the profound truth that your words and
thoughts matter to God. You can actually bring him pleasure with what
comes out of your mouth and what goes on in your heart. We will soak
in this rich verse each day this week. Today, notice one of the names for
God: He is your Redeemer. You were in danger, and he rescued you. You
were a slave, and he purchased you and set you free. The fact that the all-
powerful, all-perfect God is listening to what you say and probing into
your deepest thoughts sounds absolutely terrifying — until you remember that he loves you so much that he paid the price for your pardon.
God is your Redeemer.

LIVE THE WORD

Write down the words of Psalm 19:14, and carry them with you or
put them in a prominent place where you will see them regularly. Pray
these words regularly this week.

WEEK 4: MOUTH AND MIND

DAY 2

LISTEN TO THE WORD

May these words of my mouth and this meditation of my heart be
pleasing in your sight, LORD, my Rock and my Redeemer.
(Psalm 19:14)

The prayer of Psalm 19:14, and indeed all of our prayers, are
addressed to a God who is described here as a "Rock." He is not some
wimpy, wavering deity who can be shaken by circumstances; he is Rock
solid and unimaginably strong. And notice what the verse says. He is not
just any ol' rock; he is your Rock. He is the source of your strength. He
is the firm place for you to stand. He is the fortress where you can find
protection. God is your Rock.

LIVE THE WORD

Are things unstable in your life right now? Pray to God your Rock,
and ask him to help you stand on him.

DAY 3

LISTEN TO THE WORD

May these words of my mouth and this meditation of my heart be
pleasing in your sight, LORD, my Rock and my Redeemer.
(Psalm 19:14)

Your words have tremendous power. They can be used to build
someone up or to bulldoze them. With a single sentence, you can make
someone's day. With another kind of sentence, you can cause a sleepless
night. You can use words to call attention to how good God is, or you
can use words to try to impress people with how good *you* are. According
to Psalm 19:14, your words are so powerful that they can even bring
pleasure to God. Every phrase you utter reaches his ears, and what you
say today can put a smile on God's face.

LIVE THE WORD

Before you move on to today's next task, use words to encourage
someone. Walk across the room, make a phone call, or write a note or an
email. Pray that those words will be pleasing in God's sight, and that they
will lift up the one who receives them.

Day 4

Listen to the Word

May these words of my mouth and this meditation of my heart be
pleasing in your sight, LORD, my Rock and my Redeemer.
(Psalm 19:14)

God is intently tuned in to what is going on inside you. He wants
to find things that please him in "the meditation of (your) heart." The
word translated "meditation" literally means "muttering." What are the
mutterings of your heart? What are the things that your mind repeatedly
returns to, the things you turn over and over, the things you intentionally dwell on and obsess about? God wants you to soak your mind in
thoughts that bring life to you — thoughts that are pleasing in his sight.

Live the Word

God is your Rock and your Redeemer — seek to hold that truth
before your mind as often as possible today. Let that reality be the meditation of your heart.

WEEK 4: MOUTH AND MIND

DAY 5

LISTEN TO THE WORD

May these words of my mouth and this meditation of my heart be
pleasing in your sight, LORD, my Rock and my Redeemer.
(Psalm 19:14)

As we pray Psalm 19:14, we are expressing our hope that what we
do will be pleasing in God's sight. This prayer provokes an important
question: whom are you living to please? Often the words of our mouths
are used to try to be pleasing in the sight of other people, seeking to
demonstrate to them how smart, or how funny, or how spiritual, or how
powerful we are. Often the meditation of our hearts centers on how we
can improve our public approval ratings. Through this prayer, we invite
God to set us free from our need to impress other people. We tell him
that his opinion is the only one that matters.

LIVE THE WORD

Make plans to do a good deed this weekend that no one else will ever
know about. Perhaps you could bathe someone in prayer without telling them, or deliver an anonymous gift, or do some secret act of service.
Don't seek credit for your good deed from anyone else; keep it between
you and God.

Week 5: Transformation

WEEK 5: TRANSFORMATION

DAY 1

LISTEN TO THE WORD

…He who began a good work in you will carry it on
to completion until the day of Christ Jesus.
(Philippians 1:6)

If you had stumbled upon Michelangelo crafting his famous statue of David in the early stages of his work on the project, my guess is that you would not have been overly impressed. You would probably see nothing more than a big stone mass with a few chunks knocked out of it. But if you told the artist that his sculpture more closely resembled Jabba the Hut than it did the biblical king, he would no doubt pass along some important information: it isn't finished yet!

Neither are you. Like the statue, you are an unfinished masterpiece. You may be disappointed with much of what you see in yourself right now. But the Artist who is shaping you has some important news: he isn't finished with you yet. And he will not quit. He will complete the work of forming you into the person he wants you to become.

LIVE THE WORD

Thank God for his unceasing effort to craft you into a masterpiece. Ask him to help you cooperate with him this week as he forms and transforms you.

DAY 2

LISTEN TO THE WORD

And we all, who with unveiled faces contemplate the Lord's glory,
are being transformed into his image with ever-increasing glory....
(2 Corinthians 3:18)

Paul tells us what your life will look like when the divine Artist is finished with the masterpiece that is you: you will look like Jesus. You "are being transformed into his image." Jesus is the prototype; he is the pattern God is using as he forms you. God doesn't want to settle for making you a little nicer, or furnishing you with a little more courage, or giving you a little more joy. His plans are much more impressive. He wants you to be just like Jesus.

LIVE THE WORD

As you go through the day today, pray this "breath prayer" as often as it comes to mind: "Lord Jesus, make me like you."

WEEK 5: TRANSFORMATION

DAY 3

LISTEN TO THE WORD

Not that I have already obtained all this, or have already arrived
at my goal, but I press on to take hold of that for which
Christ Jesus took hold of me.
(Philippians 3:12)

Philippians 3:12 makes it clear that your spiritual transformation requires a kind of partnership between you and God. It is both something you take hold of and something that takes hold of you. Of course God does the heavy lifting. No matter how hard you try, you cannot engineer your own righteousness. Only God can change you and make you like him. But you have an active role to play. You don't just sit around and hope God waves a magic wand and makes you suddenly Christ-like. You must "press on" and "take hold of" what God is offering you. You must actively cooperate with him as he works to transform you. You must take steps to place yourself in his hands so he can shape you. You must pursue him as he pursues you.

LIVE THE WORD

As an act of cooperation with God in his work to transform you, commit Philippians 3:12 to memory.

WEEK 5: TRANSFORMATION

DAY 4

LISTEN TO THE WORD

…Train yourself to be godly. (1 Timothy 4:7)

Most of us could not run a marathon today, no matter how hard we tried. It just isn't in us. If we wanted to be able to run a marathon, we would have to enter a life of training that included proper routines of exercise, rest, and nutrition. The right training routine would reshape our bodies and make us capable of doing something we are currently unable to do. The key to success in distance running is not trying hard — it is training well.

The same is true in spiritual growth. We assume that the key to becoming like Christ is to try really hard: I will do my best to be compassionate, joyful, patient, and so on. But no matter how hard we try, we fail. It just isn't in us. If we want to be like Jesus, we must enter a life of spiritual training. If we rearrange our lives around spiritual exercises like prayer, worship, soaking in Scripture, fellowship, solitude, and service, God uses those practices to develop our spiritual muscles and make us capable of living as Jesus would live if he were in our place.

LIVE THE WORD

As an act of spiritual training, declare a fast. Choose something you normally enjoy as a part of your daily life (perhaps food, or television, or the Internet), and choose to refrain from experiencing it for the rest of this day. Ask God to use this exercise to show you that he is the only thing you can't live without.

DAY 5

LISTEN TO THE WORD

…"Can I not do with you, Israel, as this potter does?" declares the Lord. "Like clay in the hand of the potter, so are you in my hand, Israel."
(Jeremiah 18:6)

God is the most gifted, creative sculptor imaginable, and you are clay in his hands. As you cooperate with him, he is shaping you into a masterpiece. He is forming you into something that is beautiful and useful to him. Many people strive to be self-made pots, deciding for themselves what they will become and attempting to form themselves. That kind of project doesn't generally turn out very well. Things go much better when we place ourselves in God's hands and trust him to mold us, refine us, and shape us into the pattern of Jesus Christ.

LIVE THE WORD

When a small annoyance or inconvenience comes your way today, don't get upset about it or try to take control of the situation. Receive it as something that God has allowed to come your way, and ask him to use it as part of his process of transforming you into the likeness of Jesus.

Week 6: Satisfaction

WEEK 6: SATISFACTION

DAY 1

LISTEN TO THE WORD

You, God, are my God, earnestly I seek you; I thirst for you, my whole being longs for you, in a dry and parched land where there is no water... I will be satisfied as with the richest of foods.

(Psalm 63:1, 5)

How satisfied are you? On a scale of one to ten, how would you rate yourself? Let's say ten means you are completely content, you have all you need, you wouldn't change anything and you wouldn't trade places with anyone. And let's say one means you are totally unsatisfied, you hate your life, and you think there are probably forms of algae that have it better than you. Where on the scale are you?

We often live with a sense that something is missing. We spend a ton of energy trying to fill up on all the wrong things. The Scripture we will explore this week reminds us that only God can quench our deepest thirst and satisfy our ultimate hunger.

LIVE THE WORD

If your satisfaction score is low, ask God to show you what wrong things you are trying to fill up on. Ask him to persuade you that true satisfaction can only be found in him.

DAY 2

LISTEN TO THE WORD

You, God, are my God, earnestly I seek you; I thirst for you, my whole
being longs for you, in a dry and parched land where there is no water...
I will be satisfied as with the richest of foods.

(Psalm 63:1, 5)

Do you sense that something is just not right? You feel like you need
more. Maybe you're not even sure what you need more of, but you know
you need more. There is an empty spot inside you. If you stay busy, you
can ignore it for a while. But in your quiet moments, you know it is
there. Sometimes it keeps you up all night. Sometimes it keeps you down
all day.

The psalmist says you live in a dry and parched land where there is
no water. There are many things around you that promise to satisfy, but
they all turn out to be mirages. They leave you empty and thirsty.

Nothing in this world can give you what you are craving. Only God
can truly satisfy.

LIVE THE WORD

Read today's Scripture aloud, emphasizing the word "you" each time
it occurs. Ask God to remind you that he is the One you must seek to
find satisfaction.

DAY 3

LISTEN TO THE WORD

You, God, are my God, earnestly I seek you; I thirst for you, my whole
being longs for you, in a dry and parched land where there is no water...
I will be satisfied as with the richest of foods.

(Psalm 63:1, 5)

Physical hunger and thirst have symptoms that are easily identi-
fied. So do spiritual hunger and thirst. When your stomach is not full, it
growls. Likewise, when your soul is not full, it also growls.

Sometimes your spiritual dissatisfaction shows up in a grouchy mood
— you blow up over stuff you should blow off. Sometimes it comes out
in chronic complaining, or continual disappointment in your relationships. Sometimes it rears its head through envy and resentment. Other
times you may experience an outbreak in the area of one of your pet sins.
All of these indicators point to a spiritual emptiness — a hole that needs
to be filled with God.

LIVE THE WORD

Do you see any symptoms of spiritual emptiness in your life today?
Confess those things to God, and ask him to fill your emptiness with
himself.

DAY 4

LISTEN TO THE WORD

You, God, are my God, earnestly I seek you; I thirst for you, my whole
being longs for you, in a dry and parched land where there is no water...
I will be satisfied as with the richest of foods.

(Psalm 63:1, 5)

I love how our psalm describes the experience of having our emptiness filled by God: "I will be satisfied as with the richest of foods." God
fills us up! And we're not talking TV dinner here. We're not talking low
salt, low fat, low carb, low flavor food substitutes. We're talking real food!
The good stuff. Filet mignon, fettuccini Alfredo, homemade bread with
real butter, chocolate cake — the richest of foods! God satisfies us, and
he does it right!

LIVE THE WORD

Pray the words of today's Scripture.

DAY 5

LISTEN TO THE WORD

You, God, are my God, earnestly I seek you; I thirst for you, my whole
being longs for you, in a dry and parched land where there is no water...
I will be satisfied as with the richest of foods.

(Psalm 63:1, 5)

What do you long for? What are you thirsty for? Whether you know
it or not, the thing you crave is God. You may label it as something else.
But only God has what you really desire. Only he can give you a sense of
purpose bigger than yourself. Only he can provide peace that will withstand the pressures of your life. Only he can offer you a jumbo-sized joy
that circumstances cannot shrink. Only he can satisfy.

LIVE THE WORD

Ask God to fill you with himself and give you the satisfaction that
only he can give.

Week 7: Risk

WEEK 7: RISK

DAY 1

LISTEN TO THE WORD

Then they said to the king, "Daniel, who is one of the exiles from
Judah, pays no attention to you, Your Majesty, or to the decree you put
in writing. He still prays three times a day."
(Daniel 6:13)

We place a high value on being comfortable and safe, but the Bible
commends many people who did something reckless for God. This week
we will investigate the connection between faith and risk.

Daniel took a big risk for God. The king passed a law forbidding
prayer to anyone but himself, making it clear that anyone who broke
that law would become lion lunch. Daniel kept right on praying to God
anyway. He put his life on the line, refusing to alter his pattern of regular
communication with God. We know the end of the story — we know
that God rescued Daniel from the lions. We often say that Daniel was
rescued from the lions' den because of his faith, and that may be true.
But of course it was also his faith that got him thrown into the lions' den
in the first place! When was the last time your faith led you to take a risk
that got you in trouble?

LIVE THE WORD

Ask God to stretch you this week and make you more willing to take
a risk for him.

DAY 2

LISTEN TO THE WORD

Then Caleb silenced the people before Moses and said, "We should
go up and take possession of the land, for we can certainly do it."
(Numbers 13:30)

Caleb was one of twelve spies sent to do some reconnaissance work
in the land God wanted to give his people. All twelve saw the same good,
fertile land that would make an ideal home for the people. All twelve
also saw walled cities and well-armed soldiers who weren't exactly roll-
ing out the welcome mat. Most of the spies said that claiming the land
would be impossible — that they would be squashed like bugs if they
even tried. Caleb said they should load up the U-haul trucks and move
in immediately. Why was Caleb willing to take such a risk? Simply put,
Caleb knew that God was with them and he wanted them to have the
land. Caleb knew it was better to be out on a limb with God than to be
"safe" on the ground away from him. Unfortunately the majority won
out. God's people didn't go in to the land, and they spent the next forty
years wandering in the wilderness and wondering, "what if?"

LIVE THE WORD

Think of a time when you settled for what you thought was the safe
route and things did not turn out very well. Ask God to use that memory
to help you take the risk of going his direction in the future.

Day 3

Listen to the Word

Calling his disciples to him, Jesus said, "Truly I tell you,
this poor widow has put more into the treasury than all the others.
They all gave out of their wealth; but she, out of her poverty,
put in everything — all she had to live on."
(Mark 12:43–44)

One day Jesus sat in the temple with his disciples, watching folks give their offerings. A wealthy businessman in a designer suit dropped in a check for $1000, and Jesus yawned. A landowner signed over the deed to a prime piece of real estate, and Jesus drummed his fingers and looked bored. Then a poor widow gave two small copper coins, worth less than a penny, and Jesus stood up and applauded. He made the astounding statement that she had given more than all the others.

How remarkable that the giver that Jesus chooses to hold up for us as an example is a woman who gave a gift that wouldn't even buy a piece of bubble gum. He brags on her not because she gave the most, but because she gave all. She trusted God enough to take the risk of giving a reckless offering.

Live the Word

Ask God what kind of reckless gift he might want you to give him through your church.

DAY 4

LISTEN TO THE WORD

Jesus looked at him and loved him. "One thing you lack," he said.
"Go, sell everything you have and give to the poor, and you will have
treasure in heaven. Then come, follow me." At this the man's face fell.
He went away sad, because he had great wealth.
(Mark 10:21–22)

Jesus offered a huge challenge to a man we have come to know as the rich young ruler. That description of him lets us know that he had three of the things our world thinks are important — wealth, youth, and influence. But Jesus knew that there was still something lacking, and he knew just the answer. The man needed to follow him. But to be able to give his ultimate allegiance to Jesus, he would have to let go of the stuff that currently occupied first place in his heart. Jesus asked the man to give away his possessions to help the poor, giving God the opportunity to replace his love for money with a love for heavenly treasure.

Unfortunately, the man decided that parting with his wealth was too much of a risk. He held on to his pile of cash, but he missed the golden opportunity to live life as a disciple of Jesus.

LIVE THE WORD

Ask God to help you identify something you treasure that prevents you from following Jesus well. Ask him what he wants you to do about it.

DAY 5

LISTEN TO THE WORD

"Come, follow me," Jesus said, "and I will send you out to fish for people." At once they left their nets and followed him.
(Mark 1:17–18)

Jesus found some fishermen in a boat and offered them a promotion: follow me, and you can start fishing for people. And they followed him at once! They left their nets, walking away from their careers and from life as they knew it. He didn't even tell them where they would be going. Still, they took the risk of following him.

Jesus extends the same call to us: "Follow me! Go where I lead you. Live as I instruct you. Follow me." Answering that call is still a risk. It involves leaving some familiar things behind. We don't know everything the journey will hold or everywhere it will take us. Will you follow? Will you follow at once?

LIVE THE WORD

Is there an area of your life where your obedience to Christ has been less than immediate? Ask him to help you follow him "at once" in that matter.

Week 8: Savoring Scripture

WEEK 8: SAVORING SCRIPTURE

DAY 1

LISTEN TO THE WORD

Keep this Book of the Law always on your lips; meditate on it day and
night, so that you may be careful to do everything written in it.
Then you will be prosperous and successful.
(Joshua 1:8)

Imagine that you are Joshua. You are on a really big bus with a couple
million cranky refugees. The bus is parked right on the border of the
Promised Land, next to a big "No Trespassing" sign, and it is finally time
to go in and claim what God wants to give you. Moses has been driving
the bus for forty years, but Moses is dead. God has just handed you the
keys. He has given you perhaps the most impossible leadership challenge
in the history of ever: to take over for the guy who parted the Red Sea,
delivered the law, and provided bread from heaven. God knows you are
more nervous than Colonel Sanders' pet chicken, but he tells you the key
to being prosperous and successful in the task before you: meditate on
the Book.

Meditating on Scripture was crucial for Joshua, and it is crucial for
you. This week we will learn about this vital practice.

LIVE THE WORD

Commit Joshua 1:8 to memory.

DAY 2

LISTEN TO THE WORD

Keep this Book of the Law always on your lips; meditate on it day and
night, so that you may be careful to do everything written in it.
Then you will be prosperous and successful.
(Joshua 1:8)

Meditating sounds like something complicated or confusing or
weird. We have all kinds of wrong ideas associated with the word — we
envision a monk in a monastery, or some flake sitting on a hillside in the
lotus position saying "ohhhmmm" and becoming one with the grass or
reconnecting with his inner infant or something.

But meditating on Scripture is not complicated or confusing or
weird. It is simply filling your mind with Scripture, paying sustained
attention to the Bible. You may think you don't know how to meditate,
but if you know how to worry, you know how to mediate. To worry is
to take a negative thought and marinate in it, turning it over and over in
your mind. To meditate on Scripture is to turn it over and over in your
mind, savoring it, pondering it, working on it and letting it work on you.
Scripture meditation is something you can do — something you must do.

LIVE THE WORD

Choose a short verse of Scripture (Psalm 23:1 or Philippians 4:13
would do nicely) and spend a few moments pondering what it means,
and what it means *to you.*

DAY 3

LISTEN TO THE WORD

Keep this Book of the Law always on your lips; meditate on it day and
night, so that you may be careful to do everything written in it.
Then you will be prosperous and successful.
(Joshua 1:8)

What do you expect to happen when you read Scripture? Do you
expect that you will learn some new facts about the Moabites, or get a
Magic 8 Ball-style answer to a problem, or just be able to check it off
your to-do list?

How about encountering the God who made you? How about hearing the voice and knowing the heart of your heavenly Father? God wants
you to meet him in the pages of the Bible. The Bible is more than a
book, more than a passive object for you to study. It is "living and active"
(Hebrews 4:12). Through what you read, God may just step into the
mess of your world and offer words of wisdom or comfort or confronta-
tion or whatever it is that you need. You should expect that to happen.
Approach the Bible anticipating an encounter with God.

LIVE THE WORD

Each time you read the Bible this week, begin your reading by asking
God to meet with you in what you read.

DAY 4

LISTEN TO THE WORD

Keep this Book of the Law always on your lips; meditate on it day and
night, so that you may be careful to do everything written in it.
Then you will be prosperous and successful.
(Joshua 1:8)

Do you read the Bible for information or for transformation? The
first approach simply asks questions of the text; the second approach also
allows the text to ask questions of you. The first approach attempts to
cover as much material as possible; with the second approach, you might
choose to stay in a holding pattern over words or phrases that are working
on you. The goal of the first approach is to get through the Scripture; the
goal of the second approach is to get Scripture through you. If you are
reading for information, you hope to master the Bible. If you are reading
for transformation, you hope to let the Bible master you.

Learning is good, but don't settle for learning. Go for life change.
Joshua 1:8 challenges you to meditate on God's Word so you can *do* God's
Word. Approach Scripture seeking transformation, not just information.

LIVE THE WORD

Choose a key passage of Scripture (perhaps Ephesians 6:10–20 or
Colossians 3:1–17). Take your time reading the passage, asking God to
challenge you and change you through what you read.

WEEK 8: SAVORING SCRIPTURE

DAY 5

LISTEN TO THE WORD

Keep this Book of the Law always on your lips; meditate on it day and
night, so that you may be careful to do everything written in it.
Then you will be prosperous and successful.
(Joshua 1:8)

There is a problem with our usual approach to Scripture. We have a
ten-minute "quiet time" during which the Bible is working on us. But for
the other 23 hours and 50 minutes of the day, we are on our own. Joshua
1:8 challenges us to take Scripture with us — to "meditate on it day and
night." That doesn't mean that we are always locked in a room with a
Bible in our lap. It means that as we go through life, we are continually
reflecting on Scripture, continually allowing it to shape our thoughts and
actions.

There are many ways you can apply this instruction. You can write a
verse of Scripture on a card and put it in your pocket. You can put Post-It
notes with Scripture on them in prominent places in your daily path. You
can memorize verses (that's not just for kids in Vacation Bible School!).

Scripture meditation does not have to be separate from the rest of
life. It is something you can do day and night.

LIVE THE WORD

Joshua 1:9 promises: "the Lord your God will be with you wherever
you go." Make a conscious effort to repeat that promise to yourself as
often as possible today.

WEEK 9: CONFLICT

Week 9: Conflict

Day 1

Listen to the Word

If your brother or sister sins against you, go and point out their fault,
just between the two of you. If they listen to you,
you have won them over.
(Matthew 18:15)

You could change the "if" at the beginning of this week's Scripture to a "when." It is going to happen. Someone in your life is going to offend you. You will experience conflict. That conflict may take the form of open hostility, or simmering resentment, or just a growing distance between you and the other person. But if you are in relationships, you can count on some conflict. This week we will examine Jesus' practical instruction for addressing that conflict.

Jesus challenges us to acknowledge the problem and take action. The central command of his instruction is "go." Don't stick your head in the sand and ignore the obvious. Don't dodge the person or the issue. Don't pretend the conflict is okay. Look the problem square in the eye and deal with it. Go to the other person and do the hard work required to make things right.

Live the Word

Have you experienced conflict with someone recently? Spend a moment praying for that person, and for your relationship with them.

DAY 2

LISTEN TO THE WORD

If your brother or sister sins against you, go and point out their fault,
just between the two of you. If they listen to you,
you have won them over.
(Matthew 18:15)

When there is conflict in a relationship, Jesus challenges you to be the one to own responsibility and take the initiative for reconciliation. He says it is your job to seek to make things right. We don't like to do this. We get caught up in assigning blame, and we wait for the other person to admit their fault. But in this week's Scripture, Jesus says though the other person is the one who has sinned, you are the one responsible to work toward restoration.

Interestingly, in Matthew 5:23–24, Jesus describes a situation in which *you* have caused offense and are apparently the one at fault. In that case he says it is also your responsibility to take the initiative to reconcile the relationship. Whether you are the person in the wrong or the victim (and in most situations of conflict you will be a little bit of both), Jesus tells you to take responsibility for making things right.

LIVE THE WORD

Ask God to give you the courage to take the initiative in healing a damaged relationship.

WEEK 9: CONFLICT

DAY 3

LISTEN TO THE WORD

If your brother or sister sins against you, go and point out their fault,
just between the two of you. If they listen to you,
you have won them over.
(Matthew 18:15)

When we find ourselves in conflict with someone, Jesus clearly instructs us to go directly to the person involved. That is usually the last person we want to approach. It is more fun to go to someone else and say, "I just want to get some objective feedback from a neutral third party. Here's what has happened... Now don't you agree that this other person is a deeply disturbed, possibly psychopathic loser?" Sometimes we go to another person really looking for help or accountability, but usually we are just looking for an ally — for someone to reinforce our conviction that we are a mistreated martyr and the other person is the antichrist.

Instead of rehearsing our anger with a third party, Jesus challenges us to go to the person with whom we have the conflict. We don't need to get more people lined up against that other person — we need to get that person and ourselves back into a healthy relationship.

LIVE THE WORD

If someone comes to you today and badmouths another person, gently encourage them to go directly to the other person to resolve the issue.

DAY 4

LISTEN TO THE WORD

If your brother or sister sins against you, go and point out their fault,
just between the two of you. If they listen to you,
you have won them over.
(Matthew 18:15)

Jesus approaches the issue of conflict resolution with his customarily perfect blend of grace and truth.

He says, "Go and point out their fault." Don't dance around the issue. Be direct. Don't get fuzzy and say part of what concerns you and hope they will fill in the blanks and figure out the rest. Speak the truth clearly.

But he also says to discuss things "just between the two of you." This is a reminder to be sensitive in the way you approach them. There is no need to make a public announcement of the flaws of the other person. There is no need to embarrass them by forcing them to respond in front of an audience. Don't just toss the "truth" out there like a grenade. Jesus would have you deal with the other person as you would want them to deal with you — with grace.

LIVE THE WORD

Which is harder for you to demonstrate in situations of conflict — grace or truth? Ask God to grow that trait in you.

WEEK 9: CONFLICT

DAY 5

LISTEN TO THE WORD

If your brother or sister sins against you, go and point out their fault,
just between the two of you. If they listen to you,
you have won them over.
(Matthew 18:15)

Notice the goal of Jesus' teaching on conflict resolution. What is the desired outcome? The ultimate aim is not to score points, or to put the other person in their place, or to get something off your chest. The goal is not to make them realize how wrong they were and how right you were. It is not to fix them or punish them. The objective is to restore the relationship, to "win them over." Reconciliation is the whole point.

Reconciliation is the only legitimate reason to have this kind of difficult conversation with someone. If you aren't ready for reconciliation, then you aren't ready to confront the other person about the offense — the conversation will just lead to more conflict. If you just want to win the fight, things will stay ugly between you and the other person. But there is hope if you join God in working toward reconciliation.

LIVE THE WORD

Ask God to make you aware of anyone he wants you to approach to seek reconciliation of a relationship, and ask him to give you the strength for any difficult conversations that may be necessary.

WEEK 10: GOD IS STRONG

WEEK 10: GOD IS STRONG

DAY 1

LISTEN TO THE WORD

Be exalted in your strength, LORD; we will sing and praise your might.
(Psalm 21:13)

God deserves our worship for more reasons than we could count. This week, we will follow the instruction of Psalm 21:13 and praise him specifically for his might. We will celebrate the limitless strength of God.

God is powerful enough to create everything out of nothing. He is great enough to lead a nation of slaves to freedom, tossing in a few dozen miracles along the way. He is strong enough to use Joshua's trumpets to topple Jericho's walls, and to use David's sling to topple Goliath. He is mighty enough to turn a crucifixion into a resurrection. God is strong!

LIVE THE WORD

Praise God for his strength. Ask him to open your eyes to his might this week, in these devotionals and in your daily life.

DAY 2

LISTEN TO THE WORD

When Abram was ninety-nine years old, the LORD appeared
to him and said, "I am God Almighty; walk before me
faithfully and be blameless."
(Genesis 17:1)

God appeared to elderly Abraham and introduced himself as "God
Almighty." The Hebrew behind that name is El Shaddai. It is a name that
highlights the limitless strength of God. God wanted Abraham (and you)
to know that there are no boundaries to his ability. There are no problems
that are too much for him, no challenges too tough for him to tackle.
There is nothing he can't do! The God you worship is God Almighty.

LIVE THE WORD

Is there a problem before you that seems like it may be more than
even God can handle? Lift that problem to him, and ask him to work in
a way that confirms his might.

WEEK 10: GOD IS STRONG

DAY 3

LISTEN TO THE WORD

And God said, "Let there be light," and there was light. (Genesis 1:3)

God's might was on clear display in creation. He simply spoke everything into existence. He announced that he wanted it to happen, and it happened. He said, "Let there be light," and there was light. He said, "Let there be llamas," and there were llamas! And he made it all out of nothing. Perhaps you could build something, but you would need materials with which to build. You couldn't construct something out of thin air. But God took nothing and made everything. He didn't just shape some pre-existing stuff. There was no stuff to be shaped until God said, "Let there be stuff!"

LIVE THE WORD

Take a look out your window and notice something God created. Ponder for a moment the power that was required to design and build what you see.

DAY 4

LISTEN TO THE WORD

Lift your eyes and look to the heavens: Who created all these?
He who brings out the starry host one by one and calls forth
each of them by name. Because of his great power and mighty strength,
not one of them is missing.
(Isaiah 40:26)

Consider the "great power and mighty strength" required to create our sun. Every second of every day and night, the sun creates 13 million times more energy than the entire population of the United States uses in an entire year. How much energy must the One who created that sun possess? And our sun is just one average star among the billions of stars he created in our galaxy, which is just one of the billions of galaxies he made. The One who created and ignited all those stars is incomprehensibly strong. He is the Mighty God!

LIVE THE WORD

Let the sun be your cue to ponder God's power today. Each time you notice its rays, praise God for his infinite strength.

WEEK 10: GOD IS STRONG

DAY 5

LISTEN TO THE WORD

Finally, be strong in the Lord and in his mighty power. (Ephesians 6:10)

Contemplating the limitless power of God can make us feel pretty small. Who are we compared to God Almighty, the creator of everything? But Ephesians 6:10 points us to an encouraging truth: God wants to loan you some of his might. God wants you to be strong in his strength. He makes his ability available to you. As you face the obstacles in your path today, you can plug into the infinite power of God.

LIVE THE WORD

Ask God to help you rely on his might, not your own small strength.

WEEK 11: WORRY

DAY 1

LISTEN TO THE WORD

Therefore I tell you, do not worry... (Matthew 6:25)

We will spend the next two weeks exploring some biblical teaching about worry. Today's Scripture commands us not to worry — and it may as well order us not to breathe. Worry is our favorite spiritual discipline! It is hard to imagine a life free from worry. We are anxietyaholics.

But worry is a spiritual sickness. Worry indicates that we think it is up to us to care for ourselves, provide for ourselves, and hold the universe together. It reveals that we lack confidence in God's competence — that we aren't certain that he can be trusted. Worry is the opposite of faith. It is impossible to trust God and worry at the same time — it would be like being simultaneously hot and cold. We can't be both fretful and faithful. The bottom line is that we either trust God or we worry.

LIVE THE WORD

Confess to God your tendency to worry. Ask him to help you trust more and worry less today.

Day 2

Listen to the Word

Can any one of you by worrying add a single hour to your life?
(Matthew 6:27)

Jesus makes a great point with regard to worry: it doesn't accomplish anything! You can't name a single instance in which worry was constructive. Maybe you are unhappy with your physical stature — worrying about it isn't going to add a single inch (trust me, I would know). Perhaps you are concerned about your lifespan — worrying about it isn't going to add a single hour. In fact, in light of what we know about the way worry negatively impacts the immune system, the digestive system, and the heart, it is safe to say that worry actually *subtracts* hours from life.

Someone has said that worry is about as effective as trying to solve an algebra equation by chewing bubble gum. It simply isn't helpful.

Live the Word

Pray that each time you begin to worry today, God will remind you of the uselessness of that anxiety.

DAY 3

LISTEN TO THE WORD

And why do you worry about clothes? See how the flowers of the field grow. They do not labor or spin. Yet I tell you that not even Solomon in all his splendor was dressed like one of these.

(Matthew 6:28–29)

Jesus tells us that worry is completely unnecessary because our Creator cares for his creatures. He challenges us to pay attention to creation. Notice that the flowers don't toil or spin. They don't get stressed out about the high prices and low selection at the mall. And they are clothed very well — God provides abundantly for them. Even Hollywood royalty decked out for the red carpet can't compete with a simple wildflower. In the same conversation, Jesus urges us to notice the birds — they don't get uptight about planting and reaping and storing (and I've never heard about a bird with a migraine or an ulcer). The birds just assume God will feed them, and he does.

Jesus' point is that we don't need to worry. If God cares enough to provide for birds and flowers, he will certainly care for us. We are in good hands. Worry is not necessary.

LIVE THE WORD

Take a look out the nearest window. Spend a moment observing the slice of creation that you can see, and ponder the great job God does taking care of it. Ask him to assure you that you can trust him to care for you, too.

DAY 4

LISTEN TO THE WORD

So do not worry, saying, "What shall we eat?" or "What shall we drink?" or "What shall we wear?" For the pagans run after all these things, and your heavenly Father knows that you need them.
(Matthew 6:31–32)

Jesus indicates that much of our worry comes from chasing the wrong things. We are running after the same things the world runs after. Our priorities have not yet been baptized. We are still caught with our neighbors in the game of what shall we eat/ what shall we wear/ what shall we drive/ what shall we invest/ what club should we join/ what prestigious job should we hold?

Running after these things inevitably leads to anxiety. It is impossible to focus on stuff and status and not worry, because these things can let you down. The fear of "what if" will always be in your mind. If you spend your energy chasing food, clothes, personal happiness, money, image, and other temporary things, don't be surprised when you are chronically worried. Worry is the natural result of letting the temporary overshadow the timeless — of letting the everyday crowd out the eternal.

LIVE THE WORD

What do your worries reveal about what matters most to you? Ask God to help you arrange your priorities appropriately.

DAY 5

LISTEN TO THE WORD

Therefore do not worry about tomorrow, for tomorrow will worry about itself. Each day has enough trouble of its own.
(Matthew 6:34)

We know some of the things that are coming tomorrow, and we are worried about those things. Other parts of tomorrow are a mystery, and the uncertainty we feel over that mystery also leads to anxiety. We are worried about what will happen, and we are worried about what *might* happen. Jesus makes it clear that worrying about tomorrow is completely unproductive. It will not make tomorrow's load any lighter if you start carrying it today. It will just reduce the amount of strength you have available to handle today's challenges.

Imagine a bridge. Over its lifetime, that bridge can support the weight of millions of vehicles. But it can't support all of those vehicles at once — it would collapse. Likewise, you were built to receive life one day at a time. With God's help, you have the structural strength to handle the weight that will come to you this day. You may not have the strength to handle today's load while simultaneously taking the load of tomorrow and every future day onto yourself. Worry about tomorrow tomorrow. Just deal with today's troubles today.

LIVE THE WORD

Ask God to help you put your full energy into what is before you today, not wasting any of it worrying about tomorrow.

WEEK 12: WORRY

DAY 1

LISTEN TO THE WORD

Do not be anxious about anything, but in every situation, by prayer and
petition, with thanksgiving, present your requests to God.
And the peace of God, which transcends all understanding, will guard
your hearts and your minds in Christ Jesus.
(Philippians 4:6–7)

This week's Scripture tells us that the path from worry to peace is
prayer. Prayer is the antidote to anxiety. That may sound like the most
obvious thing in the world, but we don't often put it into practice. We
tend to collect our anxieties instead of casting them on God.

What if you allowed worry to become a cue to pray? Like your body
automatically stands when you hear the national anthem, or like you
instinctively press the accelerator when the light turns green, you can
train yourself to pray as soon as the knot inside you starts to tighten.
Instead of pushing that concern inward, lift it upward in prayer. Instead
of marinating in the worry, release it to God. Give your angst an address.
Lift it to your Creator. Tell him you need him to handle it.

LIVE THE WORD

What is troubling you most right now? Stop turning it over and over
in your mind, and instead turn it over to God in prayer.

DAY 2

LISTEN TO THE WORD

Do not be anxious about anything, but in every situation, by prayer and
petition, with thanksgiving, present your requests to God.
And the peace of God, which transcends all understanding, will guard
your hearts and your minds in Christ Jesus.
(Philippians 4:6–7)

Our Scripture promises that when we pray, we will experience peace.
And not just any peace — God's peace. God has a lot of peace — he is
never worried, he has complete confidence in his own ability to run the
universe, nothing gives him ulcers. He is completely calm, and he wants
you to experience his peace.

It is a peace that transcends your understanding. A loose translation:
God's peace will blow your mind. It doesn't make sense. It is beyond
any rational explanation. Maybe you have seen it in action in a friend
who faces hardship with an inner strength you didn't know they pos-
sessed. Maybe you have experienced it yourself during a season in which
the walls are crashing down around you, yet for reasons you can't fully
comprehend, you are okay. You may not be able to figure out his peace,
but he promises that you will experience it if you come to him in prayer.

LIVE THE WORD

Ask God to replace your anxiety with his peace. Tell him you don't
need to understand it, but you desperately need to experience it.

DAY 3

LISTEN TO THE WORD

Do not be anxious about anything, but in every situation, by prayer and petition, with thanksgiving, present your requests to God.
And the peace of God, which transcends all understanding, will guard your hearts and your minds in Christ Jesus.
(Philippians 4:6–7)

Our Scripture says that when we pray, God's mind-blowing peace will stand guard over our hearts and minds. It is ironic that the passage uses a military metaphor to describe God's peace. God's peace is like a soldier on watch, standing guard over you. When worry approaches, God's peace says, "Who goes there?" points a weapon, and tells worry to get lost.

We tend to look for stuff to worry about, and we are good at it. We can find sources for anxiety in every direction. But God's peace is on watch duty, so you don't have to be anxiously scanning the horizon for new threats. God's peace has you covered. It is standing guard.

LIVE THE WORD

Spend a moment pondering the good news that God's peace is standing sentry watch over you. Relax, confident that your Lord is on the lookout.

DAY 4

LISTEN TO THE WORD

Do not be anxious about anything, but in every situation, by prayer and
petition, with thanksgiving, present your requests to God.
And the peace of God, which transcends all understanding, will guard
your hearts and your minds in Christ Jesus.
(Philippians 4:6–7)

Our Scripture calls us to pray "in every situation." God invites us to
pray all the time, as our regular habit, no matter what is going on. The
Scripture says that prayer is the path from anxiety to peace. But it isn't
telling us that praying when we are worried is the path to peace. Praying
"in every situation" is the path to peace. So the key to peace is not just
tossing up a quick prayer in the heat of an anxious moment. The key to
peace is living life in regular communication with God, praying in every
situation. If prayer is our pattern, then we will have peace.

So you don't need to wait until you are worried to pray. Make prayer
your lifestyle, not just your response to a crisis. If you pray even when you
are not worried, then you will worry less.

LIVE THE WORD

What were you doing right before you read this devotion? Spend
some time in prayer talking to God about it, whatever it was. It may not
seem like a big deal or a "spiritual" thing to discuss with God, but it is
part of the "in every situation" category about which he invites you to
pray.

WEEK 12: WORRY

DAY 5

LISTEN TO THE WORD

Do not be anxious about anything, but in every situation, by prayer and
petition, with thanksgiving, present your requests to God.
And the peace of God, which transcends all understanding, will guard
your hearts and your minds in Christ Jesus.
(Philippians 4:6–7)

What is the biggest anxiety you are carrying right now? You have a
choice about how to handle it — you can either worry about it, which
leaves it in your hands, or you can pray about it, which places it in God's
hands.

Imagine God speaking these words to you: "That load you are carrying — it is too heavy for you. I didn't design you to handle something
like that. It will crush you. Please release it. Trust me with it. You can
trust me with anything. Bring it to me in prayer. Trade it in for my peace
that transcends all understanding."

LIVE THE WORD

Spend a moment in prayer, asking God to take control of the situations that trigger your anxiety, and asking him to take control of your
anxious heart.

Week 13: Name Trashing

WEEK 13: NAME TRASHING

DAY 1

LISTEN TO THE WORD

You shall not misuse the name of the LORD your God, for the LORD
will not hold anyone guiltless who misuses his name.
(Exodus 20:7)

In the third of the Ten Commandments, God instructs us not to
trash his name. This week we will explore several ways that we tend to
violate that commandment.

Obviously, one way we misuse God's name is by using it as an exple-
tive. We have a tendency to say "O my God" or "good Lord" when
praying is the furthest thing from our minds. Imagine that you are walking barefoot in the dark, and you stub your toe. You immediately cry
out, "Oh _____!" Many different words are used to fill in that blank,
most of them unfit to say. Among the options is God's name. We are
not putting God's name in very good company. In our slang, the words
"God" and "hell" are often interchangeable — both can be said after you
stub your toe, or hit a bad golf shot, or burn the cookies. It doesn't take a
brilliant theologian to figure out that this is a problem! We should respect
God enough to respect his name more than that.

LIVE THE WORD

Ask God to help you honor his name this week with the way you
speak and the way you live.

74

WEEK 13: NAME TRASHING

DAY 2

LISTEN TO THE WORD

You shall not misuse the name of the LORD your God, for the LORD
will not hold anyone guiltless who misuses his name.
(Exodus 20:7)

The third commandment is bigger than simply a warning not to
use God's name as a curse word. The Hebrew phrase that is translated
"misuse the name" is literally, "take up the name pointlessly." God commands us not to speak his name flippantly, as if it doesn't matter.

Don't speak the name of the God of ages without realizing what you
are doing. Don't sing his name 73 times in a worship service when what
you are really thinking about is the number of light bulbs in the sanctu-
ary or the menu options for lunch. Don't just shove his name into every
gap in your prayers without thinking about the One you are addressing.
Don't say, "God bless you" to someone who sneezes when what you are
really thinking is, "Don't you dare sneeze on me, you nasty sick person."
We trash God's name when we use it casually. We must be mindful that
we are handling a precious treasure when his name is on our lips.

LIVE THE WORD

Prepare to pray by thinking about the One with whom you are
speaking. After you have become sufficiently impressed with who he is,
call his name and begin to pray.

DAY 3

LISTEN TO THE WORD

You shall not misuse the name of the LORD your God, for the LORD
will not hold anyone guiltless who misuses his name.
(Exodus 20:7)

It is actually possible to misuse God's name without even opening
our mouths. We trash God's name when our lifestyle is inconsistent with
his character. Even when we are not speaking God's name, we bear God's
name. The Bible says we are his people, called by his name. If people
identify you as God's, then you bear his name, and all you do reflects on
him.

I once heard a police officer describe the delight he took in giving
tickets for traffic offenses to people with Christian emblems on their cars.
He found it hypocritical for a vehicle to have a bumper that said, "I love
Jesus" while its speedometer said, "I ignore the law." As Christians, we
bear God's name. Every sin we commit is done with his name plastered
on us.

In a sense, the third commandment is a warning against hypocrisy
— we must not be called by his name and yet live in a way that is inconsistent with his character.

LIVE THE WORD

For the next hour, be conscious of the fact that you bear God's name.
Ask him to help you to speak and act in a way that is consistent with that
reality.

DAY 4

LISTEN TO THE WORD

You shall not misuse the name of the LORD your God, for the LORD
will not hold anyone guiltless who misuses his name.
(Exodus 20:7)

We have some pretty big names for God. We call him things like
"Lord" and "King." These titles imply that we consider him to be the
boss, that he is the one calling the shots. But are these titles descriptions
of the way things really are for us, or are they just pretty words? Jesus once
asked why we call him "Lord, Lord" but refuse to do what he says. That
is a question worth pondering.

Don't just call him "Lord." Let him actually be Lord. If you give him
the title without the authority, the words are empty. You are trashing
God's name.

LIVE THE WORD

Think back on your day so far — has there been a time when you
went your way instead of going God's way? Confess that to him, and tell
him you want to let him lead again.

WEEK 13: NAME TRASHING

DAY 5

LISTEN TO THE WORD

You shall not misuse the name of the LORD your God, for the LORD
will not hold anyone guiltless who misuses his name.
(Exodus 20:7)

God wants you to lift up his name rather than tearing it down. He
wants you to treasure it, to value it. He wants to help you live in such a
way that his name is honored. God wants people around you to notice
that when you open your mouth, what comes out tends to be truthful,
helpful, and encouraging. He wants the people who observe you when
you are facing a crisis to notice that you do so with hope and strength
that comes from him. God wants your friends to notice that your life is
marked with joy and patience and kindness and other rare virtues. When
they see these things in you, they will realize that your God really does
make a difference, and that will bring honor to his name.

LIVE THE WORD

Pray that God will cause everyone you encounter today to be
impressed with him.

WEEK 14: GOD FORGETS

WEEK 14: GOD FORGETS

DAY 1

LISTEN TO THE WORD

I, even I, am he who blots out your transgressions, for my own sake,
and remembers your sins no more.
(Isaiah 43:25)

Did you know that the Bible says there is something God doesn't know about you? Of course, God knows quite a lot about you. He knows your name; the Bible even says he has it written on his hand. He knows when you sit and when you rise, when you go out and when you lie down. He knows your words before you speak them. He knows the number of hairs on your head. He knows the plans he has for you. But there is one thing he doesn't know. I'm sure that sounds like blasphemy. But take a look at today's Scripture.

God doesn't remember your sins. What an amazing statement! That is the one thing about you that the all-knowing God refuses to know. He doesn't remember your mistakes. God is graciously forgetful.

LIVE THE WORD

Write down Isaiah 43:25 and put it somewhere that you will see it often. Commit it to memory before the end of the week.

DAY 2

LISTEN TO THE WORD

I, even I, am he who blots out your transgressions, for my own sake,
and remembers your sins no more.
(Isaiah 43:25)

The amazing promise in Isaiah 43:25 allows us to envision some conversations with God. You might pray, "God, remember the time I committed that sin, and I asked you to forgive, and you forgave?" And God answers, "Sorry, that doesn't ring a bell. I remember the forgiving part, but I'm a little fuzzy on the sin." Or perhaps you say to God, "I'm so ashamed I committed that sin so many times." And God responds, "What sin?"

You may have perfect recall of many of your past failures. You may choose to store them in the basement of your soul. But God has blotted them out. When you repent, God forgives and forgets.

LIVE THE WORD

Ask God to give you peace and assurance that your past sins are long gone, blotted out and forgotten.

DAY 3

LISTEN TO THE WORD

I, even I, am he who blots out your transgressions, for my own sake,
and remembers your sins no more.
(Isaiah 43:25)

We would expect God to remember our past sins. After all, he knows
everything. There is no limit to his knowledge. On top of that, he is
100% holy. Sin stands in such stark contrast to his perfection that we
would expect it to stick in his memory. Furthermore, sin is a slap in
his face. Each time we sin, we are declaring a coup against his loving
leadership and putting ourselves in charge. We would think God would
remember sin clearly. He certainly has the ability and the right to remember it and rub our noses in it. But he chooses to forget.

When you confess your sin to God, he forgets. He deletes the file.
He shreds the documents. He erases the board. He remembers your sins
no more!

LIVE THE WORD

Read Isaiah 44:22 and meditate for a moment on that additional
assurance of God's desire to forgive.

DAY 4

LISTEN TO THE WORD

I, even I, am he who blots out your transgressions, for my own sake,
and remembers your sins no more.
(Isaiah 43:25)

The promise of Isaiah 43:25 is astounding to us because when someone sins against us, we remember it all too well. I'm sure you remember
the time someone talked about you behind your back, or forgot your
birthday, or chose someone else over you. In fact, remembering the sins
of others is one of our specialties. We love to keep score. We are the
people of the grudge. We carry around a big sack full of offenses. We
have an outstanding memory when it comes to other people's sins. We
remember their sins forevermore.

God is different. We have done things that are inexcusable, irrevers-
ible, and intolerable. But God chooses to forgive and forget.

LIVE THE WORD

Think of someone you are having trouble forgiving for a past
offense. Ask God to help you to be as graciously forgetful as he is.

DAY 5

LISTEN TO THE WORD

I, even I, am he who blots out your transgressions, for my own sake,
and remembers your sins no more.
(Isaiah 43:25)

It is God's very nature to forgive and forget. We may imagine him shaking his head as he listens to our prayers, saying, "Tough luck. You have already confessed that same sin forty-three times. You are over the limit." But that score-keeping God is not the God of the Bible.

God introduces himself as the forgiving, forgetful God. He says, "I am he who blots out transgressions. I am he who forgets sins." He is saying, "This is my specialty — it is what I do." More than that, God is saying, "This is who I am. I am the God who blots out your sins. I do this for my own sake — it is consistent with my character. I am the Father who forgets your failures."

God has a selective memory for your good. You live in light of his forgiving forgetfulness.

LIVE THE WORD

Read the words of Isaiah 43:25 aloud, and envision God speaking them personally to you.

WEEK 15: TEMPTATION

WEEK 15: TEMPTATION

DAY 1

LISTEN TO THE WORD

When tempted, no one should say, "God is tempting me." For God cannot be tempted by evil, nor does he tempt anyone; but each person is tempted when they are dragged away by their own evil desire and enticed. Then, after desire has conceived, it gives birth to sin; and sin, when it is full-grown, gives birth to death.

(James 1:13–15)

We will spend the next two weeks reflecting on temptation. This week, we will begin with an obvious truth from James 1:14 — "each person is tempted."

To be human is to be tempted. Every person alive has moments when the wrong path looks really inviting, when we feel our heart start to resonate with a harmful option before us. Even if we want to be people who consistently say "yes" to God, there are so many competing offers out there, and sometimes we are drawn to them. And though God can work in our hearts in such a way that certain temptations aren't as appealing as they once were, we will never be spiritually bulletproof. Learning to handle temptation is a critical skill for the follower of Christ. Each person is tempted.

LIVE THE WORD

Which wrong path is most tempting to you today? Ask God to give you the wisdom and strength you need to be able to avoid it.

DAY 2

LISTEN TO THE WORD

When tempted, no one should say, "God is tempting me." For God
cannot be tempted by evil, nor does he tempt anyone; but each person
is tempted when they are dragged away by their own evil desire and
enticed. Then, after desire has conceived, it gives birth to sin; and sin,
when it is full-grown, gives birth to death.

(James 1:13–15)

Our Scripture starts with instruction that seems unnecessary at first
glance: don't blame God for tempting you. We know that God is holy
and opposed to sin — of course he wouldn't tempt us, right? But we do
sometimes point a finger at him after we fall. "God, if you wouldn't have
made me this way…" Or maybe we do something that rates a 100 on the
stupid scale, which makes a big mess, and then we get mad at God for
letting us do it. James makes it clear that we can't blame God when we
are nabbed by temptation.

James won't even let us get away with blaming the people around us,
or the media, or even the Devil. He points instead to our own evil desire.
He says if you want to find the main source of the problem, you need to
take a look in the mirror.

LIVE THE WORD

Have you tried to pass the blame for a recent failure? Confess that to
God, and acknowledge to him that your failure was your responsibility.

DAY 3

LISTEN TO THE WORD

When tempted, no one should say, "God is tempting me." For God cannot be tempted by evil, nor does he tempt anyone; but each person is tempted when they are dragged away by their own evil desire and enticed. Then, after desire has conceived, it gives birth to sin; and sin, when it is full-grown, gives birth to death.

(James 1:13–15)

You'd have to be an extremely foolish fisherman to put some bait on your hook, then take a look at it and say, "Mmm, that looks delicious," and then swallow it down, hook and all. But James says that is exactly what we do when it comes to temptation. We bait our own hook. We let our own evil desire drag us away. The big problem is that, deep down, we intensely desire the wrong stuff.

If you struggle with alcoholism, the root of the problem is not in the bottle — it is in your heart. If you are hooked on pornography, the source of your sin is not on a Web site — it is in your heart. If you wrestle with anger, the cause is not in the people who receive your wrath — it is in your heart.

LIVE THE WORD

The problem is in your heart, so that's where the cure is needed. Ask God to change your heart, helping you to desire what he desires for you.

WEEK 15: TEMPTATION

DAY 4

LISTEN TO THE WORD

When tempted, no one should say, "God is tempting me." For God
cannot be tempted by evil, nor does he tempt anyone; but each person
is tempted when they are dragged away by their own evil desire and
enticed. Then, after desire has conceived, it gives birth to sin; and sin,
when it is full-grown, gives birth to death.
(James 1:13–15)

James gives us what we might call a genealogy of temptation: Desire
is the mother of sin, and sin is the mother of death. "Gives birth to death"
might be the most ironic, disgusting, but accurate phrase in the Bible.

There is a short and sure progression. We desire the wrong things.
That desire consistently leads to sinful actions. And the sinful action consistently leads to death. "Death" may seem like an exaggeration of the
result of sin, but I'm sure you have seen it happen. Sin can kill relationships and careers, for starters. It slaughters your self-respect. And it leaves
you spiritually lifeless, dead to the loving action of God in your life.

Your harmful desires may look appealing in the moment, but without fail, they lead to death.

LIVE THE WORD

Ask God to give you the wisdom to see the long-term disaster that
can come from flirting with unhealthy desires. Tell him you want to go
his way, which leads to life.

DAY 5

LISTEN TO THE WORD

When tempted, no one should say, "God is tempting me." For God
cannot be tempted by evil, nor does he tempt anyone; but each person
is tempted when they are dragged away by their own evil desire and
enticed. Then, after desire has conceived, it gives birth to sin; and sin,
when it is full-grown, gives birth to death.
(James 1:13–15)

James declares that your struggle with temptation is a personal one.
Your tendency to get dragged away is not God's fault. It is not your parents' fault, or your friends' fault, or Hollywood's fault. The problem is
with your own desires.

And James makes it clear that your struggle with temptation is a seri-
ous one. The consequences are literally life and death. If you chase your
harmful desires down the road, you will find that they ultimately lead to
death.

Don't try to pass the blame. And don't try to blow it off. You must
own your temptation, and you must resist it.

LIVE THE WORD

Each time a temptation seems appealing to you today, ask God to
lend you some of his strength so you can stand firm.

WEEK 16: TEMPTATION

WEEK 16: TEMPTATION

DAY 1

LISTEN TO THE WORD

No temptation has overtaken you except what is common to mankind.
And God is faithful; he will not let you be tempted beyond
what you can bear. But when you are tempted, he will also
provide a way out so that you can endure it.
(1 Corinthians 10:13)

Each phrase of this week's Scripture drips with reassurance that we can conquer our temptations. The verse begins with news that the things that tempt you are "common to mankind." You may feel like your temptation is the most diabolical, irresistible thing out there, and that there is no way anyone could possibly understand your struggles. If so, you are making a bigger deal of your temptations than they really are. Satan isn't all that creative — his bag of tempting tricks is limited. Though your temptations may be custom-designed to prey on your unique mix of longings and lackings, you aren't the only one who has faced the challenges you face. Others have withstood those temptations and lived to tell about it. If they experienced victory, you can, too.

LIVE THE WORD

Think of someone you know who has overcome a temptation that you are still battling. Ask God to help you learn from their triumph. If it is appropriate, ask that person to share some wisdom they learned in their battle.

DAY 2

LISTEN TO THE WORD

No temptation has overtaken you except what is common to mankind.
And God is faithful; he will not let you be tempted beyond
what you can bear. But when you are tempted, he will also
provide a way out so that you can endure it.
(1 Corinthians 10:13)

An unexpected reminder sits right in the middle of our verse on
temptation: "God is faithful." On its most obvious level, our struggle
with temptation is about *our* faithfulness — will we cave in to the pressure, or will we stay true to God? But the real key to overcoming the
allure of sin is not working extra hard to beef up our faithfulness, but
rather leaning on the faithfulness of God. We can overcome temptation
because he is faithful. Because he is absolutely reliable and never leaves
our side, we have all the strength we need to do right and to avoid wrong.
We can stand firm against temptation if we stand on the unshakeable
bedrock of the faithfulness of our God.

LIVE THE WORD

Acknowledge to God that your ability to withstand temptation
depends more on his strength than on yours. Ask him to demonstrate his
faithfulness by empowering you to stand firm.

DAY 3

LISTEN TO THE WORD

No temptation has overtaken you except what is common to mankind.
And God is faithful; he will not let you be tempted beyond
what you can bear. But when you are tempted, he will also
provide a way out so that you can endure it.
(1 Corinthians 10:13)

Our Scripture gives the remarkable reassurance that God will not allow a temptation we can't handle to come our way. There has never been a temptation that has attacked me that has caused God to say, "Uh oh, that one is a doozy. I wonder if Blake can stand up to it?" Every testing is pre-approved by God in light of his perfect knowledge of your strengths and shortcomings. The temptation you experience is not big enough to defeat you. The only way it can win is if you cooperate with it.

Sometimes the pressure is so great that you might wonder if God has overestimated what you can bear, but he hasn't. He knows what you can handle, and he won't make you endure an ounce more. You don't have to waste any energy wondering whether you have the capacity to overcome a temptation that comes your way: in God's strength, you do have that capability or he wouldn't have allowed the temptation in the first place.

LIVE THE WORD

What is your biggest ongoing temptation right now? In your mind, look that temptation in the eye and tell it that God says it is not big enough to get the best of you.

DAY 4

LISTEN TO THE WORD

No temptation has overtaken you except what is common to mankind.
And God is faithful; he will not let you be tempted beyond
what you can bear. But when you are tempted, he will also
provide a way out so that you can endure it.
(1 Corinthians 10:13)

Not only does God shield us from any temptation that would be too much for us — he also builds an escape hatch in all of the temptations that he allows to come our way. He will provide a way out! You may be headed toward a crash, but keep your eyes peeled for the exit ramp that God promises is there.

Picture this scene: Satan has a net he wants to throw over you. He has to go to God for permission to use that particular net. God says, "Sure, but hand that to me for a minute." Then God cuts a big hole in the net, hands it back to Satan, and tells him to go for it.

God always provides a way out.

LIVE THE WORD

The next time you feel temptation rising up to snare you, ask God to show you the way out that he has provided.

WEEK 16: TEMPTATION

DAY 5

LISTEN TO THE WORD

No temptation has overtaken you except what is common to mankind.
And God is faithful; he will not let you be tempted beyond
what you can bear. But when you are tempted, he will also
provide a way out so that you can endure it.
(1 Corinthians 10:13)

The temptations that strike us are so powerful that sometimes it seems that sin is unavoidable. But this week's Scripture makes it abundantly clear that falling to temptation is not inevitable. The pressure to sin may be intense, but obedience is always a live option for you. Other people have experienced the same temptation and survived it. God has already evaluated that temptation and determined that you have the capacity to overcome it. God has set things up so that you can't sin unless you choose to ignore his faithfulness and avoid the way out he has provided.

With God's help, you can stand against temptation!

LIVE THE WORD

Confess to God your tendency to give in to temptation without putting up much of a fight. Ask him to remind you that you really can choose to go his way.

Week 17: Relief

WEEK 17: RELIEF

DAY 1

LISTEN TO THE WORD

Come to me, all you who are weary and burdened, and I will give you
rest. Take my yoke upon you and learn from me, for I am gentle and
humble in heart, and you will find rest for your souls.
(Matthew 11:28–29)

In this week's Scripture, Jesus diagnoses our disorder: "weary and
burdened." Does that sound like you? Are you harassed…tired…fraz-
zled…overworked…burned out…exhausted? Are you worn out and
weighed down?

The call of Jesus does not come to the perfect and put together. He
doesn't say, "Come to me, all who have it made." He invites those of us
who are struggling to make it. He invites you, with your overflowing
to-do list, your gnawed fingernails, your looming deadlines, and your
personalized set of headaches. He calls you to take your stressed-out self
to him!

LIVE THE WORD

Write out this week's Scripture and post it somewhere prominent.
Read it again each time you feel tired or anxious.

DAY 2

LISTEN TO THE WORD

Come to me, all you who are weary and burdened, and I will give you rest. Take my yoke upon you and learn from me, for I am gentle and humble in heart, and you will find rest for your souls.

(Matthew 11:28–29)

Jesus makes a remarkable promise in our Scripture: "I will give you rest." Then he repeats the promise a few seconds later when he says, "You will find rest for your souls."

Jesus offers just what we need: a chance to slow down, de-stress, and take a break. He offers relief. He gives us the opportunity to let go of our heavy, wearying burden, and to exchange it for his burden, his yoke, which he says is easy and light. Sometimes we worry that if we really give ourselves to Christ, it will be just one more big thing on our plate, one more responsibility to mess up, one more heavy burden to bear. But Jesus says he will give us rest.

LIVE THE WORD

What is your biggest source of anxiety today? Give it to Jesus in prayer.

DAY 3

LISTEN TO THE WORD

Come to me, all you who are weary and burdened, and I will give you rest. Take my yoke upon you and learn from me, for I am gentle and humble in heart, and you will find rest for your souls.
(Matthew 11:28–29)

Jesus gives three commands along with his remarkable promise of rest. These commands mark the path toward experiencing the relief he wants to give. The first command is simply, "Come to me."

The key to handling your stressed-out life is not to come to bed, or to come to vacation, or to come to a time management class, or to come to retirement. The key is not to come to religion, or to church, or to the Bible. Jesus says, "Come to ME." Only he can provide true rest. Rest and relief are gifts at the disposal of Jesus. He calls you not only to give him your heart, but to give him your burdens and your baggage. Bring it all to him, and he will give you rest.

LIVE THE WORD

Tell Jesus that you want to spend this day with him. Ask him to give you the rest that he promises to those who come to him.

DAY 4

LISTEN TO THE WORD

Come to me, all you who are weary and burdened, and I will give you rest. Take my yoke upon you and learn from me, for I am gentle and humble in heart, and you will find rest for your souls.
(Matthew 11:28–29)

One of the commands Jesus gives as part of his prescription for dealing with our weary and burdened condition is, "Take my yoke upon you." A yoke is what ancient people would put on an ox so they could make it go where they wanted it to go. In a sense, Jesus is asking you to let him take the steering wheel. He wants you to accept his authority over you.

A yoke is often a symbol of slavery and oppression. But Christ's yoke is something desirable. He is the master carpenter, so his yoke is "easy" — it fits. It was made for you. More accurately, you were made for it. You were built for life surrendered to Christ. You were engineered to be less than satisfied apart from him. You were designed to depend on Christ, and you will never really rest until you do.

LIVE THE WORD

You can probably find evidence in your life today that things don't go well when you are not submitting to Christ's authority. Confess that to him, and ask him to help you trust him with everything.

DAY 5

LISTEN TO THE WORD

Come to me, all you who are weary and burdened, and I will give you rest. Take my yoke upon you and learn from me, for I am gentle and humble in heart, and you will find rest for your souls.
(Matthew 11:28–29)

The final command Jesus gives as the path to rest is "learn from me." You are invited to learn how to live from the undisputed master of life — to enroll in school with the ultimate Teacher. Jesus wants you to learn from the rhythm of his life, from his priorities, from his prayers, from his trust, from his teachings. He wants you to sit at his feet and learn.

Resting is something we aren't innately very good at. It is a learned skill. We have to be taught how to do it. And Jesus wants to teach us how to rest in him.

LIVE THE WORD

Have you ever intentionally committed to being a student of Jesus, to learning from him how to live? If not, make that commitment to him right now.

WEEK 18: LOVE

WEEK 18: LOVE

DAY 1

LISTEN TO THE WORD

If I speak in the tongues of men or of angels, but do not have love, I
am only a resounding gong or a clanging cymbal. If I have the gift of
prophecy and can fathom all mysteries and all knowledge, and if I have
a faith that can move mountains, but do not have love, I am nothing. If
I give all I possess to the poor and give over my body to hardship that I
may boast, but do not have love, I gain nothing.
(1 Corinthians 13:1–3)

Love may be the thing our world talks about the most and under-
stands the least. We will spend the next two weeks walking through 1
Corinthians 13, seeking to understand God's perspective on love.

The chapter begins with the claim that love is absolutely indispensable. It gives us what amounts to a mathematical equation: supernatural
speaking ability plus profound spiritual insight plus extreme intelligence
plus powerful faith plus generous self sacrifice minus love equals zero. It
doesn't matter how talented you are, or how morally upstanding you are,
or how committed you are — apart from love, it is all worthless. The
absence of love is not a minor problem in life, a little pothole in your
spiritual path. Without love, you are nothing.

LIVE THE WORD

Tell God that you agree with him that nothing you can do matters
without love. Ask him to form his love in you.

WEEK 18: LOVE

DAY 2

LISTEN TO THE WORD

Love is patient... (1 Corinthians 13:4)

1 Corinthians 13 steps all over our toes with its first description of love: love is patient. Right off the bat we see that God's perspective on love is different from the world's perspective. The world describes love as a fickle, unpredictable thing. The world says you don't really choose love, it chooses you — kind of like the flu! The world says love is just something you fall into unexpectedly — and you can fall out of it just as easily.

God says that love doesn't give up so easily. Real love is patient. It doesn't fade away when the person we love isn't acting very lovely. It doesn't bail out at the first sign of trouble. It remains true even when the person we love gets on our nerves or makes silly mistakes. Love puts up with a lot. Love is patient.

LIVE THE WORD

Is there someone in your life who is difficult to love? Ask for God to help you choose to love that person with great patience.

DAY 3

LISTEN TO THE WORD

...Love is kind... (1 Corinthians 13:4)

The world says love is something you FEEL — it makes your heart race, your stomach turn flips, and your insides turn to goo. God says love is something you DO. It expresses itself in kind actions that you perform for others. Love is sharing your umbrella. It is offering a listening ear. Love is wiping a child's nose a hundred times a day and reading the same book to him for the hundredth time. Love is giving a lift to someone who doesn't have a car. It is paying a compliment to a discouraged co-worker or giving a big tip to a frazzled waitress. Love makes somebody else's problem your problem. Love is kind.

LIVE THE WORD

Ask God to bring someone to mind who needs to experience love today. Make a plan to do a specific, kind action for that person today.

DAY 4

LISTEN TO THE WORD

Love... does not boast, it is not proud. (1 Corinthians 13:4)

Pride and love are 180 degrees from one another. Pride says, "I really am somebody special!" Love says, "YOU really are somebody special!" Pride causes me to focus on myself; love requires that I put myself aside and focus on the needs of others.

Ironically, we often do "loving" deeds as an attempt to feed our pride. We give a gift or offer a service, but what motivates us is a desire for applause from others. We do a good thing for someone else so we will get credit for it. But real love is not concerned with getting credit, because real love is not proud.

LIVE THE WORD

Do something kind and loving today, but keep it anonymous. Don't allow anyone to give you credit for the good deed.

WEEK 18: LOVE

DAY 5

LISTEN TO THE WORD

Love is not rude. (1 Corinthians 13:5, NIV '84)

Some cultural observers say that rudeness is the most striking attribute of modern society. Words like "please" and "thank you" and "yes ma'am" are dropping out of our vocabulary. Blaring horns and offensive gestures are taking their place. Rudeness is an epidemic.

Sadly, we are often most rude to those we know best. We are most unloving to those we supposedly love most. The Bible says that love is not rude. It is polite and considerate. It does not take others for granted or treat them as objects to be used — it treats them with dignity and respect.

LIVE THE WORD

Have you been rude to a loved one lately? Apologize to that person today.

WEEK 19: LOVE

WEEK 19: LOVE

DAY 1

LISTEN TO THE WORD

Love… is not self-seeking. (1 Corinthians 13:5)

1 Corinthians 13 gives us several descriptions of God's kind of love. One of those descriptions comes close to summing up the entire chapter: love is not self-seeking.

Our nature is to look out for number one. "What's in it for me?" seems to be the most important question. We seek our own happiness, our own pleasure, and our own fulfillment. But love asks us to put the needs of others above our own. The New Testament word for love is *agape*. *Agape* is a self-giving love, a sacrificial love. It is a radical choice to seek what is good for others instead of obsessing about what is good for you. Love is not self-seeking.

LIVE THE WORD

Write the words "others first" somewhere prominent, and let those words remind you not to be self-seeking this week.

DAY 2

LISTEN TO THE WORD

Love... is not easily angered. (1 Corinthians 13:5)

What does it take to make you mad? How much provoking is necessary before you fly off the handle? The Bible says love is not easily angered. It doesn't have a quick trigger.

When you are in a relationship with someone, they will regularly do things that are unpleasant to you. Relationships require thick skin — you have to choose that you will not go ballistic over the least little thing. A quick temper is more than a bad habit or an inconvenient character flaw. It is a sin. It is the opposite of love. God knows that a short fuse is as lethal in relationships as it is in war, so he calls us to demonstrate a love that is not easily angered.

LIVE THE WORD

When something frustrating happens today, take a deep breath and say a quick prayer. Ask God to help you to be slow to become angry.

Week 19: Love

Day 3

Listen to the Word

Love… keeps no record of wrongs. (1 Corinthians 13:5)

We enjoy keeping score. We keep a mental list of all the things that bug us about someone, and we are always prepared to add to that list. We notice when someone does something we don't like, and we remember it in case we need it for future ammunition.

But love keeps no record of wrongs. Love doesn't hold a grudge. Love forgives. Love has a healthy spiritual amnesia, forgetting about past offenses rather than dragging them out again and again. Love treats others like God treats us, showering us with mercy and second chances.

Live the Word

Do you feel resentment toward someone who has hurt you? Ask God to help you let go of that offense and forgive.

WEEK 19: LOVE

DAY 4

LISTEN TO THE WORD

Love... always perseveres. Love never fails... (1 Corinthians 13:7–8)

Our culture views love as something that comes and goes. If "you've lost that lovin' feeling" — well, there's really nothing you can do about it. According to the world, you can fall out of love when the going gets tough.

The Bible has a different viewpoint. According to the Bible, love with an expiration date isn't real love. Real love is constant. It doesn't come and go with our moods or fluctuate according to how the other person is treating us. It is a commitment that is kept no matter what. It is permanent. It never dies and you can't kill it. Love ALWAYS perseveres. Love NEVER fails.

LIVE THE WORD

Thank God for his unfailing love for you, and ask him to develop that same loyalty in your love for others.

Week 19: Love

Day 5

Listen to the Word

…The greatest of these is love. (1 Corinthians 13:13)

Love is the core of God's character. The Bible goes so far as to say that God IS love. It is his essence. It defines who He is. And God wants love to define who we are as his children. Love is God's highest priority for your life. It is the most important thing he wants you to get right. If you don't have love, it doesn't matter if your words can move the masses. If you don't have love, it doesn't matter if you have all the answers, or if you have enough faith to make a mountain do jumping jacks. If you don't have love, it doesn't matter if you lead the nation in charitable contributions. Love matters most. Love is the greatest.

Live the Word

Pray this prayer repeatedly today: "Lord, help me love like you do."

WEEK 20: NUMBERED DAYS

WEEK 20: NUMBERED DAYS

DAY 1

LISTEN TO THE WORD

Teach us to number our days, that we may gain a heart of wisdom.
(Psalm 90:12)

Have you noticed how relentlessly time moves? Calendar pages keep flipping. Kids keep getting older. Time keeps marching. And it only marches one direction — from "once upon a time" toward "happily ever after" — and there is no rewind button. We will never have this moment again. We blink, and it is gone.

Our Scripture this week is a prayer asking God to grant us the wisdom that comes from pondering our brevity. There are important lessons God will teach us if we are willing to wrestle with the transient, fleeting nature of our existence on earth and hold it up to him.

Life is short. To be blunt: we will be dead soon, so we need to really live. We must make every moment count.

LIVE THE WORD

Commit today's Scripture to memory. Use it as a prayer throughout the week.

DAY 2

LISTEN TO THE WORD

Teach us to number our days, that we may gain a heart of wisdom.
(Psalm 90:12)

It is wise to recognize that we have a limited supply of days on earth. If we recognize that truth, we will realize that every moment matters.

Imagine that you win a gift certificate for a free vacation to your favorite place in the world. The only catch: you only get to be there for two days. I bet you would make the most of every single moment. You would want to be sure that none of that precious time was wasted.

In reality, you have been given an amazing gift — life on earth — but you only get to experience it for a limited time. If you had a life expectancy of a few millennia, maybe you could afford to waste a little time. But you've just got a few decades. You've got to stop acting like you've got all the time in the world. Every moment matters!

LIVE THE WORD

Ask God to remind you that there is no such thing as an "ordinary" moment in your day today. Every moment is a priceless gift from him.

DAY 3

LISTEN TO THE WORD

Teach us to number our days, that we may gain a heart of wisdom.
(Psalm 90:12)

Numbering our days reminds us of how small we are. Physicists and astronomers calculate that our universe is 13.7 billion years old (give or take a week or two). If you are a little above average, you get to live 80 years of that.

Let's try to visualize how brief your life is in the scheme of the history of the universe. Imagine a timeline representing that 13.7 billion years that stretches the 2500 miles from Los Angeles to New York. On that timeline, your 80 years would be a little less than an inch. Makes you really feel like something, huh? We are momentary creatures. No wonder David said, "The span of my years is as nothing before you" (Psalm 39:5).

Numbering our days is very much a humility-inducing exercise!

LIVE THE WORD

Confess to God the silliness of living as if you were the center of the universe. Admit to him that he is much bigger than you are!

DAY 4

LISTEN TO THE WORD

Teach us to number our days, that we may gain a heart of wisdom.
(Psalm 90:12)

When we number our days, we realize how small we are. But we also appreciate how big God is. We have only been around for a blink, but God has been around forever. Back in the dark ages, when telephones had chords and televisions had three channels and "tweeting" was something birds did, God was God. Back when Socrates was spouting profound things in Athens, God was God. Back when T-Rex was chasing Triceratops, God was God. Before creation, before the timeline of the universe began, God was God.

He was God long before you showed up, and he will still be God long after you make your exit. He is eternal. He is enormous.

LIVE THE WORD

Think of a challenge before you that seems especially huge. Place it in the hands of your infinitely big God, and ask him to help you trust him with it.

WEEK 20: NUMBERED DAYS

DAY 5

LISTEN TO THE WORD

Teach us to number our days, that we may gain a heart of wisdom.
(Psalm 90:12)

Numbering our days reminds us of our need for the eternal God. When we come face to face with the temporary nature of our life on earth, we yearn for something that will last. We need something constant, enduring, eternal.

I went snorkeling last summer, and I caught a hermit crab. I removed my mask and used it as a small bucket to transport the crab back to shore. The whole way back to shore, the crab was striving to get out of the mask. It was as if he realized he was made for more than that tiny space, and he was longing for the vastness of the ocean. We are not so different from that crab. As we ponder the brevity of our lives, something awakens in us that says, "Surely I was made for more than this." We long for eternity.

Our days on earth are limited. But if we connect with the everlasting God, we can receive everlasting life.

LIVE THE WORD

Ask God to help you live today in light of the fact that you were designed to live with him forever. Ask him to help you focus on things that will last.

WEEK 21: COURAGE

WEEK 21: COURAGE

DAY 1

LISTEN TO THE WORD

Have I not commanded you? Be strong and courageous.
Do not be afraid; do not be discouraged, for the Lord your God
will be with you wherever you go.
(Joshua 1:9)

Who were some of your childhood heroes? The Lone Ranger was one of mine. No outlaw was ever a match for him. He would always save the day and leave folks wondering, "Who was that masked man?" Captain Kirk was another hero — boldly going where no man had gone before, with his phaser and his yellow polyester shirt — no Klingon too tough and no challenge too big. What grabbed me most about those two was their courage. Courage is what makes a hero a hero.

Could you use a little courage? Do you wrestle with fear? Are you afraid of failure? Of certain people? Of the future? Of the past coming back to bite you?

For the next two weeks, we will seek to find courage from God that is bigger than all of our fears.

LIVE THE WORD

Read Joshua 1:9 aloud, and imagine God speaking those words to you as a personal challenge and promise.

DAY 2

LISTEN TO THE WORD

Have I not commanded you? Be strong and courageous.
Do not be afraid; do not be discouraged, for the Lord your God
will be with you wherever you go.
(Joshua 1:9)

The words in our Scripture were first spoken to Joshua at a pivotal moment in the history of the people of God. Moses had just died, and his aide and sidekick Joshua had assumed leadership of the people. Joshua was stepping into some impossibly large shoes. Imagine trying to replace Moses — Red Sea parting, law giving, manna providing, face glowing Moses. To the people, it must have felt like trying to replace Batman with Robin. And Joshua faced the massive challenge of leading an army of grouchy ex-slaves in a military campaign against entrenched, well-armed enemies.

I'm sure you have some challenges in your path, just as Joshua did. The same God who promised to be with Joshua also promises to be with you. The same God who filled Joshua with strength and courage wants to fill you. Will you trust him as Joshua did?

LIVE THE WORD

Commit Joshua 1:9 to memory.

Week 21: Courage

Day 3

Listen to the Word

Have I not commanded you? Be strong and courageous.
Do not be afraid; do not be discouraged, for the Lord your God
will be with you wherever you go.
(Joshua 1:9)

Our Scripture mentions two different approaches to life: "strong and courageous" or "afraid and discouraged." Which approach do you see when you look in the mirror? Many folks see option number two.

The Hebrew word for "afraid" describes a paralyzing fear that keeps us on the sidelines of life. "Discouraged" literally refers to an absence of courage, a courage vacuum, a complete lack of hope. These may be your words. When you look at your bank balance, or the TV news, or the brokenness around you and inside you, perhaps "terrified and discouraged" pretty much covers it.

It doesn't have to be that way. God wants to be with you, and he wants to fill you with strength and courage.

Live the Word

Ask God to give you his courage as you face the challenges of this day.

WEEK 21: COURAGE

DAY 4

LISTEN TO THE WORD

Have I not commanded you? Be strong and courageous.
Do not be afraid; do not be discouraged, for the Lord your God
will be with you wherever you go.
(Joshua 1:9)

Let's try a little imagination experiment. Think of the thing you fear the most — the biggest, hairiest, scariest monster in your life. Now picture you and that beast in a boxing ring, preparing for one on one combat. It's a terrifying image, isn't it?

But hear God say that that's not the way it is. "The Lord your God will be with you wherever you go." Picture him in the ring with you — the God who ignited the sun and scooped out the Grand Canyon. Imagine him hiding you behind himself and wiping the floor with that thing that frightens you. Notice how the big hairy monster you fear compares to your bigger, stronger God.

Your life may be filled with battles, but you do not fight them alone. The Lord, the Mighty Warrior, is with you.

LIVE THE WORD

Take your biggest fear and lift it to God in prayer. Ask him to fight for you.

DAY 5

LISTEN TO THE WORD

Have I not commanded you? Be strong and courageous.
Do not be afraid; do not be discouraged, for the Lord your God
will be with you wherever you go.
(Joshua 1:9)

You look at your circumstances and see dozens of dangerous land-mines ready to explode. You look in the mirror and see a hundred ugly flaws. You look at your calendar and see a thousand scary "what ifs." You have more than enough reasons to be afraid and discouraged.

You have only one reason to be strong and courageous: because the Lord your God will be with you wherever you go. And that is enough.

Wherever you go, God will be with you. Whatever you face, God will face it with you.

LIVE THE WORD

Each time you begin to feel worry or fear today, ask God to remind you of his presence with you.

WEEK 22: COURAGE

WEEK 22: COURAGE

DAY 1

LISTEN TO THE WORD

So do not fear, for I am with you; do not be dismayed,
for I am your God. I will strengthen you and help you;
I will uphold you with my righteous right hand.
(Isaiah 41:10)

God speaks to us through Isaiah, giving us a call to courage. He gives us five remarkable fear-busting promises. Promise #1: God says, "I am with you." You can be fearless, not because you will never face hard times, or because you are so talented or smart or well dressed or spiritual, or because the stock market is secure. You can be fearless because you are not alone. God is with you.

If you try to face the challenges of life on your own, fear is an inevitable consequence. If you face those challenges alongside the God of the universe, fear is pointless.

Don't be afraid, for he is with you!

LIVE THE WORD

Commit today's Scripture to memory, asking God to use it to remind you that you don't have to be afraid.

DAY 2

LISTEN TO THE WORD

So do not fear, for I am with you; do not be dismayed,
for I am your God. I will strengthen you and help you;
I will uphold you with my righteous right hand.
(Isaiah 41:10)

God makes several fear-busting promises in Isaiah 41:10. His second promise is this: "I am your God." This may be what you need to hear more than anything else. Perhaps you need to have a little conversation with God that goes something like this...

God: Who am I?

You: You are God.

God: Right. And who are you?

You: Um — I'm NOT God. It is not all up to me. You are the One running the universe, and you are with me. So I don't need to fear. I can have courage.

Don't be afraid, for he is your God!

Live the Word

Confess to God the pride that is behind your tendency to act like it is all up to you. Ask him to remind you that he's on the throne, and you aren't, and that things work much better that way.

Week 22: Courage

Day 3

Listen to the Word

So do not fear, for I am with you; do not be dismayed,
for I am your God. I will strengthen you and help you;
I will uphold you with my righteous right hand.
(Isaiah 41:10)

God's third fear-busting promise in Isaiah 41:10 is this: "I will strengthen you." That is a remarkable assurance. The all-powerful Creator wants to loan you some of his strength.

Imagine an empty glove. It is a weak and useless thing. All it can do is sit on a shelf. But a glove with a hand in it — that has some strength. A glove with a hand can accomplish a lot. Likewise, you alone don't have the strength to handle much. But you, filled with the strength of Almighty God, are capable of great things.

Don't be afraid, for he will strengthen you!

Live the Word

Admit to God that your strength is not adequate for the challenges you face, and ask him to follow through on this promise to fill you with his strength.

DAY 4

LISTEN TO THE WORD

So do not fear, for I am with you; do not be dismayed,
for I am your God. I will strengthen you and help you;
I will uphold you with my righteous right hand.
(Isaiah 41:10)

"I will help you." That is God's fourth fear-busting promise to you in Isaiah 41:10.

I bet you would be terrified by the task of landing an airplane – unless an experienced pilot was in the chair beside you offering to help. If you had to cook a gourmet meal for your boss, you'd be pretty intimidated, but not if your favorite Food Network stars were there to lend a hand. You'd have a hard time lifting a 200-pound box by yourself, but you could do it easily with assistance from a group of NFL offensive linemen.

Likewise, the thought of facing the challenges in your life alone may cause heart palpitations. But God — the infinitely strong, limitlessly wise, boundlessly loving God — promises to help.

Don't be afraid, for he will help you!

LIVE THE WORD

Take God up on his offer to help. Ask him to assist you with a difficult task that is before you today.

Week 22: Courage

Day 5

Listen to the Word

So do not fear, for I am with you; do not be dismayed,
for I am your God. I will strengthen you and help you;
I will uphold you with my righteous right hand.
(Isaiah 41:10)

God's final fear-busting promise in Isaiah 41:10 is a promise to uphold you with his righteous right hand. The word translated "uphold" literally means "hold secure." God wants you to know that he's got you, and he's not turning loose no matter what. You can't shake him, and the world can't shake you free from his grip. He won't fumble you. You are safe. He's holding on to you, and he'll never let go.

Don't be afraid, for he will uphold you with his righteous right hand!

Live the Word

Ponder the truth that you are held in the hand of God. Ask God to reassure you of how secure you are in him.

Week 23: God's Will

WEEK 23: GOD'S WILL

DAY 1

LISTEN TO THE WORD

"For I know the plans I have for you," declares the Lord,
"plans to prosper you and not to harm you, plans to give you hope
and a future. Then you will call upon me and come and pray to me,
and I will listen to you. You will seek me and find me
when you seek me with all your heart." (Jeremiah 29:11–13)

We will spend the week reflecting on the remarkable words of God found in Jeremiah 29:11–13. There, God announces that he has a plan for your life. He didn't create you and set you in the world and say, "I wonder what will happen to this one. This should be interesting to watch." When you arrived, God said, "I've got big plans for this one!" He has a particular outcome in mind for your life. He formed you with that goal in mind, and he works in your circumstances to achieve that goal. Think about that — the God of the universe doesn't see you as just a face in the crowd of billions of people on the planet. He knows you personally, and he has specific plans for you.

LIVE THE WORD

Read today's verses aloud. Imagine that God is speaking them directly to you.

DAY 2

LISTEN TO THE WORD

"For I know the plans I have for you," declares the Lord,
"plans to prosper you and not to harm you, plans to give you hope
and a future. Then you will call upon me and come and pray to me,
and I will listen to you. You will seek me and find me
when you seek me with all your heart." (Jeremiah 29:11–13)

God has a plan for you, and it is a good plan. He intends to prosper you and not to harm you, to give you hope and a future. In the New Testament, Paul calls God's plan "his good, pleasing, and perfect will." It is a blueprint for your future that cannot be improved upon.

God's plans for your life are better than your own. He sees more clearly than you do, and he loves you even more than you love yourself, so he is a much better planner than you are. If you could design your own future, deciding in advance all that will happen to you and all you will accomplish, it would be unwise to do it. God's plans for you are even better. He has a good plan for your life.

LIVE THE WORD

Ask God to help you live according to his plans, not your own. Pray as Jesus did in the Garden of Gethsemane: "Not what I want, but what you want."

DAY 3

LISTEN TO THE WORD

"For I know the plans I have for you," declares the Lord,
"plans to prosper you and not to harm you, plans to give you hope
and a future. Then you will call upon me and come and pray to me,
and I will listen to you. You will seek me and find me
when you seek me with all your heart." (Jeremiah 29:11–13)

It is wonderful to hear that God has a good plan for your life. We really want to know what that plan is. We would like to have a foolproof, simple method, guaranteed to reveal the will of God or your money back. But Jeremiah doesn't offer that.

Our passage of Scripture for the week does not end the way we might expect. The passage is all about God's good plans for us — how he knows those plans, and he wants us to pray to him. We would expect the passage to end with something like, "You will seek my plans, and you will find them." Instead, it says, "You will seek ME and find ME." We are obsessed with knowing God's plan. The bigger priority to God is that we know HIM.

LIVE THE WORD

Do you ever try to use God just to try to discover what his plans are? Confess that to him, and ask him to help you seek him more than you seek his plans.

DAY 4

LISTEN TO THE WORD

"For I know the plans I have for you," declares the Lord,
"plans to prosper you and not to harm you, plans to give you hope
and a future. Then you will call upon me and come and pray to me,
and I will listen to you. You will seek me and find me
when you seek me with all your heart." (Jeremiah 29:11–13)

After assuring you that he has good plans for you, God invites you to seek HIM instead of merely seeking his plans. Often, when you do that, you will also find God's plans in the process.

If you asked me to order your food for you at a restaurant, I couldn't do it. I don't know you well enough to know your preferences — I don't know what your will would be regarding a meal. But if someone in my family asks me to order for them, it is no problem. I eat with them often, so I know what they like and what they don't like. Knowing their will is a natural byproduct of knowing them. Likewise, the more you spend time with God and get to know him, the more you understand his preferences, desires, and values. Knowing his will increasingly becomes second nature to you.

When you seek God, you generally get knowledge of God's will with the package. Even when you don't, you get God, and that is enough.

LIVE THE WORD

Repeat this "breath prayer" multiple times today, as often as it comes to your mind: "Lord, I want to know you."

Week 23: God's Will

Day 5

Listen to the Word

"For I know the plans I have for you," declares the Lord,
"plans to prosper you and not to harm you, plans to give you hope
and a future. Then you will call upon me and come and pray to me,
and I will listen to you. You will seek me and find me
when you seek me with all your heart." (Jeremiah 29:11–13)

God has good plans for you, and he wants you to seek him. But the seeking he desires is not a casual, half-hearted thing. He wants you to go after him with all you've got.

Most people are *interested* in God. Few people are *passionate* about God, yearning to know him. Perhaps you are seeking God with part of your heart — you want God AND you want to be successful, or popular, or married. God doesn't promise that you will find him that way. But he guarantees that you will find him if you desire him more than anything else, seeking him with all your heart.

Live the Word

What other things are you seeking that tend to slow down your pursuit of God? Turn those things over to him and ask him to help you seek him with all your heart.

WEEK 24: COMPLAINING

Week 24: Complaining

Day 1

Listen to the Word

Do everything without complaining or arguing.
(Philippians 2:14, NIV '84)

We will spend the week reflecting on a verse of Scripture that warns us against the opposite of giving thanks: complaining.

Complaining is everywhere. You hear complaints coming from the people you live with, the people you work with, and the people you go to church with. On rare occasions you may even hear them coming from the area between your own nose and chin! We think it is our right to complain. If we don't like something, well, somebody's gonna hear about it! After all, doesn't the Declaration of Independence say we all have a right to life, liberty, and the pursuit of crabbiness? We think complaining is normal and necessary.

But God says complaining is sin. God says there is no griping allowed. God says, "Do everything without complaining."

Live the Word

With no excuses, be honest with God about your tendency to complain. Agree with him that it is a sin, and ask him to help you turn away from it this week.

DAY 2

LISTEN TO THE WORD

Do everything without complaining or arguing.
(Philippians 2:14, NIV '84)

Our Scripture commands us to do EVERYTHING without complaining. Everything! That includes going to work, eating broccoli, taking a math test, sitting in traffic, visiting the dentist — everything! And before you start assuming that the author of these words just doesn't get it, that if he had to deal with all of the hardship in your life he would complain, too, you should know that that he wrote these words from a prison cell.

We think complaining is the appropriate response to circumstances that are unpleasant. When we must endure something we don't enjoy, we assume that complaining is a reflex, our automatic response. But the Bible teaches that complaining is a choice, and it is a choice we are to avoid. Do EVERYTHING without complaining.

LIVE THE WORD

Declare your world to be a complaint-free zone today. No matter what happens, choose not to complain. Give the people around you permission to remind you of that commitment and to challenge you if they hear you complain.

WEEK 24: COMPLAINING

DAY 3

LISTEN TO THE WORD

Do everything without complaining or arguing.
(Philippians 2:14, NIV '84)

Ultimately, our complaints are gripes against God. When you complain about your situation, you are grumbling against the God who oversees your situation. You may think you are griping about your spouse, or your boss, or your pastor. But at least indirectly, you are griping about God. A complaint is an insubordinate accusation that the God who is taking care of you and arranging your life doesn't know what he is doing. Something is wrong when, instead of praising God, you trash the situation in which he has placed you. A complaint is an anti-praise. We must trade griping for gratitude.

LIVE THE WORD

What area of life prompts the most complaints for you right now? Think of three things you have to be thankful for in that area, and praise God for them.

DAY 4

LISTEN TO THE WORD

Do everything without complaining or arguing.
(Philippians 2:14, NIV '84)

A key to living a life free of complaining is to learn to be grateful for imperfect gifts. Your body, your family, your home, your church, your life — they are all imperfect. You must decide whether to dwell on all that they lack, or to give thanks for the good things about them.

We assume that gratitude automatically replaces complaining when our circumstances change and the good things outweigh the bad, but that is not how it works. I have visited folks in a hospital trauma ward whose life as they knew it was over, folks who would never be physically or financially healthy again, and I've heard them say, "I'm so thankful." I have also sat in living rooms of million dollar houses and heard people with so much going for them do nothing but complain about all they are upset about. Gratitude doesn't replace griping when your circumstances change, but when your heart changes, and you learn to be grateful for imperfect gifts.

LIVE THE WORD

Give God thanks for some of the imperfect gifts in your life. Be specific.

DAY 5

LISTEN TO THE WORD

Do everything without complaining or arguing.
(Philippians 2:14, NIV '84)

Every moment of every day, if you look for it, you can find something to complain about. Every moment of every day, if you look for it, you can find something to be thankful for.

When you are sitting in church and the congregation is singing a song that is not your favorite, you can choose to get mad and maybe write a nasty anonymous note to the staff about it. Or, you can choose to look down the row and give thanks that a brother or sister with different musical tastes is encountering God. When you open your eyes in the morning, you can immediately think, "The time is too early, the alarm is too loud, the light is too bright, the kids are too obnoxious, and my knees are too achy." Or you can say, "Thanks, God, for the gift of being alive!"

Are you searching for what bugs you, or searching for things to celebrate? Are you a faultfinder or a joyfinder?

LIVE THE WORD

Be intentional about being a joyfinder for the next hour. Look for reasons to be grateful all around you.

WEEK 25: SOLITUDE

WEEK 25: SOLITUDE

DAY 1

LISTEN TO THE WORD

Very early in the morning, while it was still dark, Jesus got up, left the house and went off to a solitary place, where he prayed.
(Mark 1:35)

This week's verse reflects a key part of Jesus' pattern for living: he spent regular time alone with God. Luke 5:16 says, "Jesus often withdrew to lonely places." The Gospels describe Jesus spending time in solitude at a number of critical junctures in his life. At the beginning of his public ministry he spent forty days in the wilderness. Before calling the apostles he spent the night in a prayer retreat on top of a mountain. After he heard about the death of John the Baptist he stepped away from the crowd. When he was facing his own execution he withdrew into the seclusion of the Garden of Gethsemane. Jesus drew strength from solitude.

Just a thought — if the perfect, sinless Son of God couldn't live without regular time alone with God, maybe you shouldn't try to do so.

LIVE THE WORD

Ask God to work in you this week to cause you to crave some time alone with him.

DAY 2

LISTEN TO THE WORD

Very early in the morning, while it was still dark, Jesus got up, left the
house and went off to a solitary place, where he prayed.
(Mark 1:35)

Jesus modeled the spiritual discipline of solitude. What is solitude?
Like fasting means refraining from food, solitude is refraining from
society. In solitude, we withdraw from the endless barrage of noise and
stimulation so we can listen to the voice of God. It is more than being
alone — it is being alone with God. Solitude is giving God our undivided
attention. We drop the to-do list, turn off the cell phone (it really can be
done!), and step away from the crowd and into his presence. Solitude is
Sabbath. It is refraining from constant activity and busyness so that we
can be recharged by our Creator.

LIVE THE WORD

What are your excuses for avoiding time alone with God? Lift those
to God and ask him to help you work through them.

DAY 3

LISTEN TO THE WORD

Very early in the morning, while it was still dark, Jesus got up, left the
house and went off to a solitary place, where he prayed.
(Mark 1:35)

Solitude helps us to let God be God. Psalm 46 challenges us to be
still and know that God is God. Honestly, we can't fully know that God
is God without being still. We can't know that he is God as long as we are
busy doing his job for him, trying to run the universe. When we stop the
frantic activity and step into solitude, we learn that the universe doesn't
unravel when we unplug. You can ignore your email and text messages
for a couple of hours, and believe it or not, the world will keep right
on spinning on its axis! God does a fine job continuing to run things
without our "help." Solitude breaks us of the idolatrous assumption that
everything depends on us. It teaches us that the world does not rest on
our shoulders. God is God!

LIVE THE WORD

Make arrangements for sometime today to spend ten minutes with
God, with no interruptions or distractions.

DAY 4

LISTEN TO THE WORD

Very early in the morning, while it was still dark, Jesus got up, left the
house and went off to a solitary place, where he prayed.
(Mark 1:35)

Solitude can help us to detoxify. We live in a lethal environment.
Our society is filled with values and pressures that shape us more than
we realize. We are continually bombarded by lies: that the rat race is ultimate, that brutal violence is entertaining, that if I want it I should have it,
and so on. Romans 12 warns us of the danger of being conformed to the
pattern of this world — of letting the world squeeze us into its mold. We
often don't notice that it is happening until we withdraw into solitude.
Time alone with God helps us to gain freedom from the forces of society
that are molding us. It helps us to hear his truth, so that we are fortified
to ignore the lies that assail us every day. Withdrawing from the world
from time to time helps us to live in the world in a healthier way.

LIVE THE WORD

Spend a few minutes alone with God in prayer. Ask him to help you
to identify some ways that you have been squeezed into the world's mold.
Ask him to cleanse you and detoxify you.

DAY 5

LISTEN TO THE WORD

Very early in the morning, while it was still dark, Jesus got up, left the
house and went off to a solitary place, where he prayed.
(Mark 1:35)

When I ask people how they are doing, I hear one answer more frequently than any other: "busy." We are multi-tasking, fast-food-eating,
go-getting people. We like to be busy. Busyness makes us feel important,
and it helps us to avoid looking too closely at the heart of life. But busyness can be one of the great enemies of life with God. We can become so
rushed and distracted and preoccupied that we just skim our lives instead
of actually living them.

Solitude can set us free from the dangers of busyness. In solitude, you
can learn that there is more to you than the tasks you perform. In solitude, you can step out of the everyday and get in touch with the eternal.
In solitude, you can stop obsessing over what is urgent and spend time on
what is important. You can spend time alone with God.

LIVE THE WORD

Spend a few minutes alone with God today. When that time ends
and you go back to your daily responsibilities, ask God to help you to do
them with your eyes on him.

WEEK 26: JUDGING

Week 26: Judging

Day 1

Listen to the Word

Therefore let us stop passing judgment on one another....
(Romans 14:13)

One of the favorite hobbies of many Christian people is judging our brothers and sisters. We have a strange tendency to spend a lot of time evaluating, labeling, critiquing, and ranking one another. When someone is less than perfect, we feel it is our duty to point it out. When someone is different from us, we feel justified in assuming that they must not be doing things right. We rate one another's spiritual performance based on lifestyle, or music preference, or clothing, or denomination, or a thousand other criteria.

Romans 14:13 has one word for us: "Stop." Just quit cold turkey. Put down the grade book. Stop passing judgment. This week we will find biblical help for dealing with the sin of judging others.

Live the Word

Ask God to help you be aware of your tendency to judge others. Confess that sin to him, and ask him to set you free from it.

DAY 2

LISTEN TO THE WORD

Who are you to judge someone else's servant?
To their own master, servants stand or fall. And they will stand,
for the Lord is able to make them stand.
(Romans 14:4)

Romans 14:4 points out one of the major problems with judging others: it isn't your job! It is not up to you to evaluate someone else's servant, and that is exactly what you are doing when you judge fellow believers. They are not performing for your pleasure. God will handle the performance reviews for those who work for him — you can lay that project down.

God has not appointed you as the umpire of the Christian family. It isn't your place to declare who is out and who is safe, who is ahead and who is behind. Just take your position in the field, play your best, cheer on your teammates, and let God keep score.

LIVE THE WORD

Think of someone you have tended to pass judgment on in the past, and claim the promise at the end of Romans 14:4 for them. Ask God to help that person stand strong for him.

DAY 3

LISTEN TO THE WORD

How can you say to your brother, "Let me take the speck out of your
eye," when all the time there is a plank in your own eye?
You hypocrite, first take the plank out of your own eye, and then you
will see clearly to remove the speck from your brother's eye.
(Matthew 7:4–5)

Jesus paints a hilarious picture in the Sermon on the Mount. He asks
you to consider how silly it would be for you to offer to remove a speck
of sawdust from someone else's eye when you had an entire two-by-four
protruding from your own eye. You obviously couldn't see well enough
to be of any help. And to make such an offer would call attention to your
own "plank problem."

Jesus is making the point that one sinner is not qualified to pass judgment on another sinner. If you feel the need to get rid of someone's sin,
start with your own log-sized problem, not someone else's speck.

LIVE THE WORD

What is the plank in your eye right now? Confess that sin to God.
And confess the hypocrisy of acting like the sins of others are worse than
your sins.

DAY 4

LISTEN TO THE WORD

Accept one another, then, just as Christ accepted you,
in order to bring praise to God.
(Romans 15:7)

Instead of passing judgment on one another, the Bible calls us to accept one another. Instead of critiquing your brothers and sisters, God wants you to embrace them "as is." And notice the pattern today's Scripture gives for that acceptance: "just as Christ accepted you." You are full of faults and flaws, yet Jesus accepted you and welcomed you into his family. He didn't wait until you could measure up. He treated you with grace — now you must extend that same grace to others. The standard for how you treat others is not how they deserve to be treated, but how Christ has treated you.

LIVE THE WORD

Thank God for accepting you, even with all your imperfections. Ask him to help you extend that same mercy to others.

DAY 5

LISTEN TO THE WORD

Bear with each other and forgive one another if any of you has a grievance against someone. Forgive as the Lord forgave you.
(Colossians 3:13)

One of the challenges of living the Christian life is that other Christians are as messed up as you are. They are imperfect. Your natural tendency when you encounter that kind of imperfection in others is to pass judgment. God calls you instead to "bear with" others — to put up with them. And he calls you to forgive. That means you choose not to hold the imperfections of your brothers and sisters against them. It means you give them permission not to be God. It means that when they offend you, you choose to let go of it.

Don't be a critic and judge. Instead, be like your Father. Be a forgiver.

LIVE THE WORD

Ask God to help you bear with the difficult people you will encounter today. With his help, extend extra mercy to them in place of the judgment that might be your normal pattern.

Week 27: Lord's Prayer

DAY 1

LISTEN TO THE WORD

When you pray, do not be like the hypocrites, for they love to pray
standing in the synagogues and on the street corners to be seen
by others. Truly I tell you, they have received their reward in full.
(Matthew 6:5)

We will spend the next two weeks learning how to pray from the
unchallenged master of prayer. Jesus spends a significant portion of his
Sermon on the Mount dealing with the topic of prayer. He begins by
telling us how NOT to pray: don't pray in order to get human applause.
Jesus points out the sad truth that prayer can deteriorate into a performance for people. If your prayer is designed to impress people with your
piety or your profound theology, you may succeed, but that will be the
only reward for your prayer. God won't answer it — he will politely stand
aside because you really aren't even talking to him. Your Father in Heaven
is the only audience that matters when you pray. Give him your full
attention, and don't worry about what anyone else thinks.

LIVE THE WORD

Find a quiet place and spend a few moments alone in prayer. Resist
the urge to report on that prayer to others — keep it between you and
God.

DAY 2

LISTEN TO THE WORD

And when you pray, do not keep on babbling like pagans, for they
think they will be heard because of their many words. Do not be
like them, for your Father knows what you need before you ask him.
(Matthew 6:7–8)

There are two people involved in a prayer — the one doing the
asking, and the One being asked. Jesus says that the pagan approach to
prayer assumes that the success of the prayer hinges on the one doing the
asking. They expect to be heard because of their words. They assume that
they must impress God by getting the words just right or going really
long, and then God will give in and grant the request.

Jesus says that the success of prayer hinges on the goodness of the
One being asked. Prayer is effective not because we get some secret for-
mula right, but because we address it to our Father, who loves us so much
that he knows what we need even before we ask him. The key is not to
pray a good prayer, but to pray to a good God!

LIVE THE WORD

Since God knows what you need before you ask him, begin your
prayers today by asking him to show you what it is that you really need.
Then ask him to grant that need.

DAY 3

LISTEN TO THE WORD

This, then, is how you should pray:
"Our Father in heaven, hallowed be your name."
(Matthew 6:9)

The model prayer Jesus gives us begins with an address. This is important — it distinguishes prayer from merely worrying out loud or making a wish. We are directing our needs and concerns in a particular direction, to a particular Person. And what a Person he is! He is "our Father" — One who cares for us and is near to us. And he is "in heaven" — infinitely above us and majestic and holy.

Jesus teaches that prayer begins with an awareness of the awesomeness of the One to whom we are praying. That puts the whole experience in perspective. We must be aware that we are talking to God, and be impressed and humbled by his greatness.

LIVE THE WORD

When you pray today, don't just dive right in to the requests you have. Begin by reflecting on the goodness and greatness of the God to whom you are praying, and be amazed!

DAY 4

LISTEN TO THE WORD

This, then, is how you should pray:
"Our Father in heaven, hallowed be your name."
(Matthew 6:9)

We don't talk about hallowing things very much these days (I had a high school teacher who referred to the "hallowed halls" of that school — that always seemed strange to me because the distinguishing feature of those halls was the presence of cockroaches large enough to have their own show on Animal Planet). But hallowed means "kept holy," or "held in high regard." We are to ask God to let his name be uniquely respected, to let it be treasured and loved more than any other. We are praying that we, and all others, will see God as he is and give him the admiration he deserves.

LIVE THE WORD

Write down some names of God (Father, Creator, Shepherd, Provider, etc.) and take a moment to praise him for who he is.

DAY 5

LISTEN TO THE WORD

Your kingdom come, your will be done, on earth as it is in heaven.
(Matthew 6:10)

I don't know about you, but my prayers often sound like letters to Santa — "I want this, I want that, give me that..." But have you ever noticed the pronouns in the first three requests of Jesus' model prayer? "Hallowed be YOUR name, YOUR kingdom come, YOUR will be done." By the end of Verse 10, the model prayer is halfway over, and we haven't asked for anything for ourselves yet. Prayer eventually moves on to our needs and wants, but first it recognizes that what WE want is not the primary issue. Jesus challenges us to pray about things that are priorities to God. Prayer is not a tool to get God on board with our agenda — he designed it so we could be a part of fulfilling his agenda!

LIVE THE WORD

What is the top item on your prayer list right now? Pray about it in a different way today, asking God to cause that situation to turn out the way he wants it.

WEEK 28: LORD'S PRAYER

DAY 1

LISTEN TO THE WORD

Your kingdom come, your will be done on earth as it is in heaven.
(Matthew 6:10)

This week we continue to consider Jesus' teaching on prayer in the
Sermon on the Mount. He instructs you to pray for God's kingdom to
come. This is a request for God to be the uncontested King of everything,
for him to be Lord of every square inch of you and every square inch of
the universe. He instructs you to pray for God's will to be done, which
is an expansion of the same idea. You are to ask that what God wants to
happen will happen in your home, your classroom, your workplace, your
neighborhood. You pray that God will reign as fully in your hometown
as he does in heaven.

LIVE THE WORD

Think of an area of your life or your world where God is not currently recognized as King. Invite him to take his rightful place there.

DAY 2

LISTEN TO THE WORD

Give us today our daily bread. (Matthew 6:11)

Jesus encourages you to ask God to supply everything you need in order to survive. If you ask God to feed you, you are acknowledging two important truths. First, you admit that you are helpless. You need him to provide for you. Second, you recognize that he cares for you. He loves you enough to get involved in meeting your needs.

It is significant that Jesus tells us to pray for bread for TODAY. We don't ask for a year's supply. We will have to pray again tomorrow for tomorrow's bread. We will have to trust God day by day.

LIVE THE WORD

Thank God for caring enough to meet your individual needs. Admit to him that you are helpless without Him.

DAY 3

LISTEN TO THE WORD

And forgive us our debts, as we also have forgiven our debtors.
(Matthew 6:12)

Jesus instructs you to ask God to forgive you. Give him your trash and ask him to get rid of it. Give him all of your hurtful words, hateful actions, and prideful attitudes, and ask him to clean you up. Be honest about your sin, and ask God not to hold it against you.

With your sin, you have accumulated a debt you could never pay. But Jesus has paid the price for you, and God yearns to forgive you. He just wants you to ask for it in prayer.

LIVE THE WORD

Do what Jesus said — confess your sin to God. Ask for and receive his marvelous forgiveness.

DAY 4

LISTEN TO THE WORD

Forgive us our debts, as we also have forgiven our debtors.
(Matthew 6:12)

If we could delete part of Jesus' model prayer, it would be the second half of today's verse. It is a little scary to pray, "God, forgive me exactly as much as I have forgiven others."

It sounds like Jesus wants us to earn God's forgiveness by forgiving others. But I believe he is simply instructing us in how forgiveness works. Those who won't give it make themselves unable to receive it. If you refuse to do your part, you cut yourself off from God's part. If you lock the door to prevent your forgiveness from going out to others, that locked door prevents God's forgiveness from getting in to you. The best way to be in the position to receive mercy is to give it regularly.

LIVE THE WORD

Have you been holding a grudge toward someone who has hurt you? For your own good, forgive that person today. What they did was wrong, but you can choose to stop holding it against them.

DAY 5

LISTEN TO THE WORD

And lead us not into temptation, but deliver us from the evil one.
(Matthew 6:13)

Jesus' model prayer closes with requests for God's protection. Jesus instructs you to make these requests because he knows that you have a nose for temptation and you would wander into every sin within a hundred miles if you were left on your own. He also knows that there is a powerful enemy working against you who would love to trip you and trap you. Jesus encourages you to admit to God that you are vulnerable and that you will be eaten alive without his help. He wants you to ask God to defend you and help you stand.

LIVE THE WORD

Ask God to steer you away from sin. Name some specific temptations, and tell him you need him to deliver you from them.

Week 29: Patience

WEEK 29: PATIENCE

DAY 1

LISTEN TO THE WORD

Be completely humble and gentle; be patient,
bearing with one another in love.
(Ephesians 4:2)

This week we will soak in some Scriptures that call us to be patient. It may not be pleasant, because patience does not come naturally for us. In fact, our whole lives are structured around impatience — we eat fast food, drive in the fast lane, and stay wired for instant communication. We want what we want, and we want it yesterday.

God sees us rushing around, skimming life as we live in a constant hurry, and he urges us to be patient. He sees us losing our temper with the people around us when they don't meet our expectations, and he urges us to be patient. Hear the words in the middle of Ephesians 4:2 as God's personal instruction to you: "Be patient!"

LIVE THE WORD

Pray a dangerous prayer today — ask God to help you grow in patience this week.

DAY 2

LISTEN TO THE WORD

Be joyful in hope, patient in affliction, faithful in prayer.
(Romans 12:12)

A bit of bad news is implied in God's instruction to be patient. If God says you are going to need patience, he is obviously assuming that you are not always going to get what you want when you want it. If everything always worked out just the way you hoped, patience would not be required. You need patience because life will be full of circumstances beyond your control. You need patience because hardships will come.

God is honest enough to warn you that life will be full of waiting rooms and traffic jams and dreams that get delayed and hopes that get dashed. Life is hard, so life requires patience.

LIVE THE WORD

What "affliction" is troubling you today? Ask God to take care of it, and ask him to help you trust him patiently as he works.

Week 29: Patience

Day 3

Listen to the Word

...Be patient with everyone. (1 Thessalonians 5:14)

One of the tough things about many commands in Scripture is their all-inclusiveness. You can probably be patient with MOST of the people around you, but today's verse won't let you be satisfied with that. It calls you to be patient with everyone. Even the annoying ones, and the demanding ones, and the smelly ones, and the mean ones, and the...

You get the picture. God asks you to be patient with everyone. Some folks require extra patience — and God calls you to provide it.

Live the Word

Pray for one of the "extra patience required" people in your life. Ask God to bless that person, and ask him to help you treat that person with patience.

DAY 4

LISTEN TO THE WORD

The Lord is not slow in keeping his promise, as some
understand slowness. Instead he is patient with you, not wanting
anyone to perish, but everyone to come to repentance.
(2 Peter 3:9)

Sometimes God seems slow. He doesn't always answer our prayers
the moment we say "amen." But when you look at things from his van-
tage point, he is not slow at all. To wait a whole day for something is a
huge burden to us. But God has been around more than a gazillion years
— waiting a day is not such a big deal to him.

Patience is one of God's primary characteristics. The fact that he puts
up with you and with me is pretty clear evidence of that! God sets the
example for us to show us how to be patient. He is patient with you. You
should return the favor by being patient with the rest of his children and
with your circumstances.

LIVE THE WORD

If you find yourself placed on hold on the telephone, or sitting in a
waiting room, or stuck in traffic or in a line at the store, ask God to use
that waiting time as patience training for you.

DAY 5

LISTEN TO THE WORD

Be still before the LORD and wait patiently for him... (Psalm 37:7)

God invites you to wait for him. He has big plans for you, and he will bring them to a flourishing finish in his timing. Wait patiently for that to happen.

Let God be God. Tell him when things aren't going your way. Tell him that not everything is happening how you want it to and when you want it to. Tell him you are not in control of things. But tell him that is okay, because you know he is in control, and you trust him. You can wait patiently because the universe is in his hands, and you are in his hands, and that is a great place to be.

LIVE THE WORD

Make arrangements to spend five minutes in silence and stillness within the next few hours. Don't try to accomplish anything — just wait patiently for God and listen for his voice.

WEEK 30: AUDIENCE OF ONE

WEEK 30: AUDIENCE OF ONE

DAY 1

LISTEN TO THE WORD

Be careful not to practice your righteousness in front of others
to be seen by them. If you do, you will have no reward
from your Father in heaven.
(Matthew 6:1)

Why do you do the good things that you do? Why do you pray and give and serve and worship? What is the motive behind your ministry? What audience is in your mind when you do spiritual things?

Jesus warns us of the danger of spiritual showoff syndrome. We often do right things for entirely wrong reasons. We seek applause from other people. Instead of doing good things for God's delight and glory, we do them so others will be impressed with us.

Discipleship should be a reality, not a performance. Jesus calls you to live for an audience of One.

LIVE THE WORD

As often as possible this week, do kind things for others in secret. Seek not to receive credit for those kind actions.

DAY 2

LISTEN TO THE WORD

Be careful not to practice your righteousness in front of others
to be seen by them. If you do, you will have no reward
from your Father in heaven.
(Matthew 6:1)

Jesus says we shouldn't expect a reward from God for acts of righteousness that we do to try to impress others. When you think about it, it makes total sense. If you pray an impressive public prayer designed to amaze the congregation with your profound spiritual insight, you aren't really talking to God. You are just putting on a show. You have chosen not to involve God, so God politely stands aside while you do your thing. The same applies for giving, and fasting, and serving, and other good deeds done for the sake of image management.

God richly rewards the things we do for him. But when we do things for the applause of people, we may get that applause, but it will be the only reward we receive.

LIVE THE WORD

As an act of secret service, pray for someone you know who is struggling. Don't tell that person or anyone else what you have done.

WEEK 30: AUDIENCE OF ONE

DAY 3

LISTEN TO THE WORD

Be careful not to practice your righteousness in front of others
to be seen by them. If you do, you will have no reward
from your Father in heaven.
(Matthew 6:1)

At first glance, this week's Scripture seems to contradict a command Jesus gives in Matthew 5:16: "Let your light shine before others, that they may see your good deeds." What is the deal?

Both verses actually address the same root problem: the tendency to worry too much about your approval ratings with the people around you — the temptation to tailor your discipleship to the expectations of others. In situations where you are inclined to downplay your connection to Christ for the sake of your image, Jesus challenges you to let your light shine. In situations where you are tempted to show off and impress others with your faith, Jesus challenges you not to do your deeds in order to be seen. In both cases, Jesus wants you to ignore the crowd and forget about what makes you look good to other people. He wants you to live naturally for him, without shame and without pretense.

LIVE THE WORD

Are you more frequently tempted to hide your faith or to show it off? Ask for God's forgiveness, and ask him to change you.

DAY 4

LISTEN TO THE WORD

Be careful not to practice your righteousness in front of others
to be seen by them. If you do, you will have no reward
from your Father in heaven.
(Matthew 6:1)

Does Jesus' command mean that no good deed has value if someone else finds out about it? Is he saying that public prayer is wrong, and that a kind deed for someone won't count in God's eyes if the person finds out that you did it?

No. The problem is not when deeds are seen. The problem is when deeds are done *for the purpose* of being seen. It is okay if someone occasionally finds out that you did a good thing. It is not okay to do the good thing in the hopes of having it discovered and praised by people. Jesus says you shouldn't expect a blessing from God if the whole project was done to impress a human audience.

LIVE THE WORD

Ask yourself a really tough question: how much of my spiritual life would be left if I took out the part done for others to see?

DAY 5

LISTEN TO THE WORD

Be careful not to practice your righteousness in front of others
to be seen by them. If you do, you will have no reward
from your Father in heaven.

(Matthew 6:1)

This week's verse raises a fundamental question for you to ponder: Whose approval do you prefer? Would you rather hear PEOPLE say, "Wow! What a strong Christian! What a prayer warrior! What a hero!" Or would you rather hear GOD say, "Well done, good and faithful servant." If you are looking for attention and applause from people, you can achieve that. If you are looking for God's approval, you can have that. The key is to be the kind of person who would rather please God than people — the kind of person who prefers the rewards God gives to the rewards that people give.

Live for your Father in heaven, and you'll have no trouble living without human applause.

LIVE THE WORD

Ask God to help you to live for his approval alone, free from concern about your image with others.

WEEK 31: SLOW DOWN

WEEK 31: SLOW DOWN

DAY 1

LISTEN TO THE WORD

Be still, and know that I am God; I will be exalted among the nations,
I will be exalted in the earth.
(Psalm 46:10)

We live life in a hurry. Our most popular restaurants are not popular because they sell nutritious food, or delicious food, or inexpensive food, but because they sell FAST food. A quick survey of my pantry at home found instant oatmeal, minute rice, and microwave popcorn — I probably could have found more, but I was in a hurry! My local phone book lists dozens of businesses with names that start with "Quick" (or "Quik," apparently indicating that they are moving so fast they don't have time for all five letters). We want everything right now!

God has a challenging word for hurried people like us: "Be still, and know that I am God." We will spend the week exploring this counter-cultural command.

LIVE THE WORD

Pay attention to the pace of your life today. Notice how many times you find yourself hurrying, and ask God to help you slow down and pay attention to Him.

DAY 2

LISTEN TO THE WORD

Be still, and know that I am God; I will be exalted among the nations,
I will be exalted in the earth.
(Psalm 46:10)

God tells you to be still because he knows that hurry is wrecking your life. Think about it: Why do you have a hard time being kind to your family? It is probably because your constant pace is go, go, go, and once you get home you are so wiped out that your family just gets emotional leftovers. Hurry is the arch-enemy of kindness, because love takes time. And what keeps you from spending time in prayer? What prevents you from being a servant to people you work with? It is probably your frantic, frazzled busyness.

God sees you whirling around and says, "Slow down. Be still. Know that I am God."

LIVE THE WORD

Take a moment to reflect on what a life of hurry is costing you. Ask God to help you live at a pace that allows you to listen to him and love others.

DAY 3

LISTEN TO THE WORD

Be still, and know that I am God; I will be exalted among the nations,
I will be exalted in the earth.
(Psalm 46:10)

"Be still." "Know that I am God." These seem to be two totally separate commands. But God knows that they are connected. He realizes that the ability to know that he is God flows from the willingness to be still. When we live our lives at warp speed, always frantically going and doing, we tend to forget that God is God. When we are constantly busy, we begin to think that we are indispensable and that the task of running the universe has fallen to us. We need to take a breath, take a break, and realize that the world keeps right on spinning without our anxious activity. We need to slow down and let God remind us that he is the one on the throne.

LIVE THE WORD

Stop what you are doing for a moment. Take a deep breath. Look for three things around you, or things that have happened so far today, that give evidence that God is God. Thank him for those things.

DAY 4

LISTEN TO THE WORD

Be still, and know that I am God; I will be exalted among the nations,
I will be exalted in the earth.
(Psalm 46:10)

You might assume that there are too many important items on your agenda for you to take time to be still. If you feel that way, I would challenge you with a simple question: are the items on your to-do list more important than those on Jesus' to-do list? Jesus was busy doing the most important work that has ever been done, yet the Gospels make it clear that he regularly took time to be still. There are multiple reports that he withdrew from the crowd to go to a mountain alone to pray. There were countless times that he reclined for a meal. He slept on a boat, and he told his disciples to get away with him for some time off. Just a thought — if the perfect Son of God benefited from regular times of stillness, maybe that practice would do you some good!

LIVE THE WORD

Confess to God the self-importance that is behind much of your hurry. Ask him to help you trust him enough to let him take care of running the universe.

DAY 5

LISTEN TO THE WORD

Be still, and know that I am God; I will be exalted among the nations,
I will be exalted in the earth.
(Psalm 46:10)

God is so convinced that being still is critical for our well being that he made it part of his original top ten list. In the Ten Commandments, he placed the call for a weekly day off right up there with instructions not to murder or worship idols. He orders us to remember the Sabbath — to establish a healthy rhythm in life that interrupts work with regular time to rest and recharge. Your car won't run forever without stops for refueling — and neither will you. You must set aside regular time to be still and know that God is God.

LIVE THE WORD

The weekend is coming — make arrangements to spend some time doing something that helps you relax and recharge. Ask God to use that time to remind you that he is God.

WEEK 32: GOD METAPHORS

WEEK 32: GOD METAPHORS

DAY 1

LISTEN TO THE WORD

A father to the fatherless… is God in his holy dwelling. (Psalm 68:5)

How can we have any idea who God really is and what he is like? How can our tiny 3-pound brains wrap themselves around the infinite God who made them? Thankfully, the Bible assists us by using some terms we can understand to describe the God who is beyond description.

One of the most remarkable descriptions of God in the Bible is that he is your Father. God chooses to reveal himself to us in terms of an intimate relationship. He is not some distant deity who couldn't pick you out of a police lineup. He cares for you even more than your parents did on their very best day. Jesus called God "Abba," which could basically be translated as "Daddy." It's the name that would be used by a first century little boy who was young enough to think his dad was the bravest, strongest, smartest, coolest person in the world. God is your loving Father, and you are his treasured child.

LIVE THE WORD

Pray to God, your Father. Thank him for revealing himself to you through the words of the Bible. Ask him to help you get to know him better this week.

DAY 2

LISTEN TO THE WORD

The LORD is my shepherd, I lack nothing. (Psalm 23:1)

The Bible frequently compares us to sheep, and that's not exactly a compliment. Sheep aren't known for being the brightest animals around. They have a hard time finding their own food, and they tend to get themselves lost rather frequently. Sheep also aren't the toughest creatures you will find (There aren't many high schools who choose a sheep as their mascot — "The Fighting Sheep" just wouldn't exactly strike fear into the hearts of their opponents). Sheep are basically defenseless against predators. A sheep left on its own would not stand a chance.

The good news is that we are not sheep who have been left on our own. We have a shepherd. The LORD is our shepherd. We don't know where to go, but he guides us. We are helpless and vulnerable, but he protects us. We can't take care of ourselves, but he provides for us.

LIVE THE WORD

Make a list of five things God has supplied for you — things you would not have been able to acquire through your own ability. Thank God for providing for you as your shepherd.

WEEK 32: GOD METAPHORS

DAY 3

LISTEN TO THE WORD

The LORD Most High is awesome, the great King over all the earth.
(Psalm 47:2)

The Bible describes God as the great King over all the earth. He has all power, and he is in command. He is the Ruler of the universe. He is sovereign over history. He reigns over the weather that is heading your way. He is the true king of the jungle, ruling over every fish that swims, every bird that flies, and every creature that creeps.

About the only place his kingship gets called into question is in our lives. Sometimes we still try to rule there. We want to call our own shots. God patiently waits for us to recognize that we are much better off when we give up our little coup attempt and let him return to the throne.

God is the great King. He rules over everything. Does he rule over you?

LIVE THE WORD

Each time you talk to God today, address him as "King." Let that understanding of his identity shape your prayers.

DAY 4

LISTEN TO THE WORD

The LORD is my rock, my fortress and my deliverer;
my God is my rock, in whom I take refuge. He is my shield
and the horn of my salvation, my stronghold.
(Psalm 18:2)

The Bible portrays God as a rock, a fortress, and a place of refuge. David, the author of Psalm 18, knew a thing or two about fortresses. He spent much of his early adulthood looking for safe places to hide while King Saul worked hard to exterminate him. David found God to be the ultimate shelter and shield. When you find yourself under attack and you are struggling to dodge all the darts that are coming your way, do what David did: run to God. Take refuge in him, and you will find strength and safety that are not attainable anywhere else.

LIVE THE WORD

What is the biggest source of fear and anxiety in your life right now? Spend a moment reflecting on how strong God is, and how the power of the thing you fear is insignificant by comparison.

WEEK 32: GOD METAPHORS

DAY 5

LISTEN TO THE WORD

The LORD your God is with you, the Mighty Warrior who saves.
He will take great delight in you; in his love he will no longer
rebuke you, but will rejoice over you with singing.
(Zephaniah 3:17)

So far this week we have seen God pictured as Father, Shepherd, King, and Fortress. The final image may be the most surprising: Scripture describes God as a singer. Zephaniah 3:17 paints a picture of God as a tender parent who holds a terrified child, singing an impromptu song to calm the child. You are the child, and God is singing over you! And notice what motivates his song: the verse says that he delights in you, and that his song is an act of rejoicing over you. God is pleased to have you as his child, and he is singing about it.

LIVE THE WORD

Now that you know that God is singing over you, why not return the favor? At your next available opportunity, sing to God of your delight in him. Choose a hymn or worship song, or compose your own spontaneous solo.

WEEK 33: WORK

WEEK 33: WORK

DAY 1

LISTEN TO THE WORD

Whatever you do, work at it with all your heart,
as working for the Lord, not for human masters.
(Colossians 3:23)

This week's verse reminds us that there must be an intersection between your faith and your work. You can't live life with your job in one compartment and your relationship with God in another. Your occupation may be as a boss or as an employee or as a homemaker or as a student. Whatever it is, Christ wants you to do it with him. If you separate your faith in Christ from your job, you are leaving him out of the place where you spend most of your waking hours. You are blocking him out of many of the relationships in your life. You are keeping him away from a primary place where your values are tested.

There must be a connection between your faith in Christ and your work. Jesus wants to go to work with you.

LIVE THE WORD

Invite God to join you at work this week. Ask him to remind you of his presence with you all week long.

WEEK 33: WORK

DAY 2

LISTEN TO THE WORD

Whatever you do, work at it with all your heart,
as working for the Lord, not for human masters.
(Colossians 3:23)

The basic instruction offered in this week's verse is simple, practical, and brilliant: Work as if Jesus were your boss. As you go through your day, act as you would act if Jesus were your boss. You don't work for the company whose name appears on your paycheck. You don't work for the man or woman whose name appears above yours on the organizational chart. You work for the Messiah, whose name is above every name!

If Jesus were the supervisor to whom you reported, what would you do differently? What would change? How would it affect your attitude? Your work ethic? Your integrity? Your workplace relationships? Your to-do list? You must do your work for Jesus, not for people.

LIVE THE WORD

Look back over the beginning of your day. What have you done that you would not have done if you had remembered that Jesus is your real boss? Confess that to him and ask for his forgiveness.

DAY 3

LISTEN TO THE WORD

Whatever you do, work at it with all your heart,
as working for the Lord, not for human masters.
(Colossians 3:23)

One of the primary ways your commitment to Christ will show up in the workplace is in the way you treat other people. Everybody you lock eyes with or speak to on the phone is someone made in the image of God. Every client, co-worker, and classmate is someone for whom Christ died.

You may tend to view a person as an annoying distraction, or a tool, or an obstacle, or a potential customer. Instead, you must view them as a child of God, or as someone God wants to adopt into his family. Each person you interact with at work matters to God. Treat them accordingly.

LIVE THE WORD

Who is someone in your workplace who could use a touch from God through you? Do something kind for that person today.

DAY 4

LISTEN TO THE WORD

Whatever you do, work at it with all your heart,
as working for the Lord, not for human masters.
(Colossians 3:23)

Your commitment to Christ will show up on the job in the quantity and quality of work that you do. If you work as if Jesus were your boss, you are going to do your best! You will "work at it with all your heart."

The Bible is full of stories of God's people who demonstrate the value of a healthy work ethic. Joseph's rise to a position of influence in Egypt happened because he worked hard and he worked with integrity. Daniel and his friends moved up the organizational chart in Babylon because they worked harder, stayed in shape better, and scored higher on the Babylonian SAT's than the people around them. You are working for Jesus, so work hard.

LIVE THE WORD

When you find yourself tempted to slack off today, get back to work — not for the sake of your company, but for the sake of Christ.

DAY 5

LISTEN TO THE WORD

Whatever you do, work at it with all your heart,
as working for the Lord, not for human masters.
(Colossians 3:23)

Your faith in Christ must impact the way you approach your job. Whether your work is high finance or heavy labor, hitting the books or doing diapers and dishes, your work can be done "for the Lord." You must work as if Jesus were your boss, because he is.

And Jesus is the best boss around. He is all-seeing, so he supervises all that you do. He conducts the only performance review that really matters. He offers a compensation and benefits package that can't be topped.

Jesus is Lord — he's the boss — so do your work for him.

LIVE THE WORD

Post the words of Colossians 3:23 somewhere that you will see them often in the days ahead. Let them remind you who your real boss is.

Week 34: Adopted

WEEK 34: ADOPTED

DAY 1

LISTEN TO THE WORD

He predestined us for adoption to sonship through Jesus Christ,
in accordance with his pleasure and will.
(Ephesians 1:5)

Do you ever wonder why you are here? Perhaps pondering the scope of our vast universe reminds you of your smallness and makes you wonder if you are just an irrelevant accident. Maybe the rut of life prompts the question of purpose for you. The day in, day out drudgery of work and school and bills and cheap thrills makes you wonder if there is a point to it all.

This week's Scripture tells you that God had a purpose in mind when he made you. He assembled you so he could adopt you! He formed you so you could become part of his family. He created you so you could be his treasured child.

LIVE THE WORD

Ask God to speak to you this week and help you embrace the purpose for which he made you.

WEEK 34: ADOPTED

DAY 2

LISTEN TO THE WORD

He predestined us for adoption to sonship through Jesus Christ,
in accordance with his pleasure and will.
(Ephesians 1:5)

You were created to be God's child. You are not an accident. Your
arrival on the scene was not a mistake or a random fluke of nature. You
were made for a reason. You were made for a relationship with God.

If you live your life apart from that relationship, you will never be
whole. You will be like a tire without air, or a lamp without a light bulb.
You will completely miss your purpose and potential. You will also spend
the rest of your life with a thirst you can't quench — a longing you can't
fulfill. You will only find significance and satisfaction if you live as God's
adopted child.

LIVE THE WORD

What are you expecting to give you significance and satisfaction
today? If it is anything other than God, confess that to him. Ask him to
show you how he can abundantly provide what you need.

DAY 3

LISTEN TO THE WORD

He predestined us for adoption to sonship through Jesus Christ,
in accordance with his pleasure and will.
(Ephesians 1:5)

The word "predestined" in this week's verse may make you nervous. The way some folks describe it, God is playing favorites, choosing some people to be his kids to the exclusion of others. It conjures up images of God playing a cruel game of "eenie, meenie, miney, moe" to decide who is in and who is out.

That is not what predestination means. The Bible tells us plainly that God does not want anyone to perish. He wants all people to have a relationship with him. And that is exactly what our Scripture tells us. He doesn't wait for people to live their lives and then determine on a case-by-case basis whether they will be welcome in his family. He predestines, he decides from the beginning, that he wants them all to be his. The New Living Translation says it well: "His unchanging plan has always been to adopt us into his own family by bringing us to himself through Jesus Christ, and this gave him great pleasure."

LIVE THE WORD

Use the phrase "I am yours, Father" as a breath prayer. Pray that prayer continually today, as often as it comes to mind.

DAY 4

LISTEN TO THE WORD

He predestined us for adoption to sonship through Jesus Christ,
in accordance with his pleasure and will.
(Ephesians 1:5)

As the father of two adopted children, I get pretty excited when I hear that God wants to adopt us as his children. That means we are chosen. It means he wants us to be HIS! It means he wants to give us a name — his name. It means he wants to provide us with a home and a family. It means he wants to give us a future.

Before you were formed, you were chosen to be God's child. Before you drew your first breath, you had a seat reserved at God's table. Before your first heartbeat, you had a place in God's heart. You were created to be the King's kid — God's treasured child!

LIVE THE WORD

Write a brief prayer of thanksgiving to God, expressing your gratitude to him for desiring to adopt you as his own.

DAY 5

LISTEN TO THE WORD

He predestined us for adoption to sonship through Jesus Christ,
in accordance with his pleasure and will.
(Ephesians 1:5)

God made you so he could adopt you into his family. Let's make two final observations about that adoption. First, see that we are adopted "through Jesus Christ." Jesus is the way into God's family. We accept our place as God's child by trusting Jesus, who lived and died and rose again for us. Second, notice the reason God wants to adopt us: "in accordance with his pleasure." Wow! It gives God pleasure to welcome you into his family! He delights to receive you, and provide for you, and protect you, and love you. He wants you to be his child because it brings him joy to be your Father!

LIVE THE WORD

Do you know someone who is not yet part of God's family? Pray that they will receive the amazing gift God has already decided he wants to give them.

Week 35: Self Control

DAY 1

LISTEN TO THE WORD

So then, let us not be like others, who are asleep,
but let us be alert and self-controlled.
(1 Thessalonians 5:6, NIV '84)

This week we will reflect on the Bible's call to practice self-control. The Greek word for self-control literally means strength or mastery. If you are self-controlled, then you have mastery over your thoughts and actions. You can make your body do what you want it to do, instead of the other way around. Instead of letting your desires and passions rule you, you rule your desires and passions. Instead of doing what FEELS good, you do what IS good.

Today's verse indicates that most people lack self-control. They sleep-walk through life as the victims of their own urges. But God doesn't want you to be like most people. He wants you to be self-controlled.

LIVE THE WORD

Invite God to work in you this week to strengthen your self-control.

DAY 2

LISTEN TO THE WORD

Therefore, prepare your minds for action; be self-controlled; set your
hope fully on the grace to be given you when Jesus Christ is revealed.
(1 Peter 1:13, NIV '84)

When you walk past the candy jar and feel a powerful chocolate craving, self-control lets you walk away without grabbing a handful. When
your alarm goes off, and everything in you would like to hit the snooze
button or throw the clock out the window, self-control empowers you to
put your feet on the floor. When you are going through the routine of
family life, and the aggravations are piling up, and you can feel the pressure gauge inside you going toward the red line, self-control enables you
to treat your frustrating family members with grace.

Self-control is the ability to choose to do what you should do even if
it is not exactly what you want to do. It is the strength to select the right
way over the easy way.

LIVE THE WORD

As a way to exercise your self-control, declare a 24-hour fast from
something you normally enjoy. You could give up television, or caffeine,
or something else you like. Pay attention to God to see what he will teach
you through the experience.

DAY 3

LISTEN TO THE WORD

Like a city whose walls are broken through is a person
who lacks self-control.
(Proverbs 25:28)

The Bible teaches that we have a sin nature. All things being equal, we tend to choose the selfish route. We are just bent that way. Giving in to temptation is the default setting of our system. But self-control lets us do a manual override of the system, choosing to do right instead of automatically doing what is wrong. When someone near you says something foolish, your natural instinct may be to say something to embarrass them. But with self-control you can keep your mouth shut. When you see an attractive person of the opposite sex, your natural instinct may be to stare and indulge in some lustful thoughts. With self-control, you can move your eyes and think about something else. You don't have to plunge into every sin that presents itself to you. You can practice self-control.

LIVE THE WORD

Confess to God a recent time you fell to temptation instead of practicing self-control, and receive his forgiveness.

DAY 4

LISTEN TO THE WORD

Be self-controlled and alert. Your enemy the devil prowls around
like a roaring lion looking for someone to devour.
(1 Peter 5:8, NIV '84)

Self-control is a form of spiritual armor. It protects us from temptation. 1 Peter 5:8 is a reminder that if we don't have the protection of self-control, the devil will eat us for lunch. Most of us have the bite marks to prove the truth of that verse. Without self-control, you are the helpless victim of a cruel and cunning enemy. With self-control, you stand a fighting chance.

LIVE THE WORD

Ask God to make you alert to temptation today. Ask him to empower you to practice self-control.

WEEK 35: SELF CONTROL

DAY 5

LISTEN TO THE WORD

But the fruit of the Spirit is… self-control. (Galatians 5:22-23)

The biggest irony about self-control is that we must lose control in order to gain it. Self-made self-control is impossible. It is not a do-it-yourself project that you can accomplish by your effort and willpower alone. True self-control is really God-control. It is the fruit of the Spirit — the byproduct of a life fully yielded to God's Spirit. The only way you can have control of your desires is if God has control of you. The only way you can consistently choose the right way over the easy way is if you have decided that above all you want to go God's way. To live a healthy life, you must have self-control. And to have self-control, you must surrender control to God.

LIVE THE WORD

Offer yourself to God as often as possible today through this breath prayer: "I'm yours, Lord."

WEEK 36: GOD THE GIVER

WEEK 36: GOD THE GIVER

DAY 1

LISTEN TO THE WORD

The Lord will indeed give what is good... (Psalm 85:12)

We could excuse God if he was the most selfish being in the universe. After all, everything that exists is rightfully his. We would understand if he chose to keep it all to himself. And when he gives something to us, we have such a tendency to abuse it, or to take it for granted, or to take credit for it — who could blame God if he chose to cling tightly to it all? But today's Scripture reveals a surprising truth — a truth that will be our theme for the next two weeks: God is a GIVER. He is incomprehensibly generous. He gives what is good.

LIVE THE WORD

Thank God for being the generous Giver of good gifts. Ask him to make you more like him.

DAY 2

LISTEN TO THE WORD

He gives strength to the weary and increases the power of the weak.
(Isaiah 40:29)

God is a giver, and he wants to give you the gift of strength.

Today's Scripture hits the bullseye with a one-word diagnosis of our condition: "weary." We face a continual onslaught of rush hour traffic, fast food, highspeed connectivity, and other features of our hurry-up world, and we are worn out.

You need strength. And you won't find it in another cup of coffee. God has all the power you need, and he longs to give it to you.

LIVE THE WORD

Ask God to give you his strength for the challenges before you today. Throughout the day, remember that you must rely on him for the power you need.

WEEK 36: GOD THE GIVER

DAY 3

LISTEN TO THE WORD

May the Lord turn his face toward you and give you peace.
(Numbers 6:26)

God is a giver, and he wants to give you the gift of peace.

Today's verse is part of the blessing the Old Testament priests were instructed to speak over God's people. It is not an accident that the blessing makes a connection between our peace and the orientation of God's face. We can be at peace because we know that God's face is turned toward us — he is constantly watching out for us. If we believe God has turned away from us and is distracted by other things, then anxiety is the inevitable result. If we were on our own to face the challenges of life, peace would be impossible. But we aren't! God's loving eye is on us, and he wants to give us peace.

LIVE THE WORD

Each time you feel anxiety creep up on you today, remind yourself that God is watching over you, and ask him to give you peace.

DAY 4

LISTEN TO THE WORD

If any of you lacks wisdom, you should ask God, who gives generously to all without finding fault, and it will be given to you.

(James 1:5)

God is a giver, and he wants to give you the gift of wisdom.

Do you ever come up short in your quest for answers? Are you ever unsure about which path to take? Today's Scripture has good news: you can ask God, and he will give you wisdom.

And notice how God gives: "generously." He is not stingy with his gifts, which is good, because we can use all the help we can get. And notice to whom God gives: "to all without finding fault." He doesn't wait for us to measure up, which is good, because he wouldn't have to look hard to find our flaws.

LIVE THE WORD

Is there a difficult decision before you this week? Ask God to give you his wisdom.

DAY 5

LISTEN TO THE WORD

I will give you a new heart and put a new spirit in you; I will remove
from you your heart of stone and give you a heart of flesh.
(Ezekiel 36:26)

God is a giver, and he wants to give you the gift of a new heart.

A heart of stone is not good for much. It stubbornly resists being
molded by the Master. It is impervious to feeling — no joy for life's
simple pleasures, no compassion for the pain of others. It is dead. But
God wants to perform a spiritual heart transplant on you. He wants to
replace your rock-hard heart with a softer one, a heart that beats with his
and responds to his touch, a heart that is fully alive.

LIVE THE WORD

Reflect on some additional verses that describe the kind of heart
God wants to give you: Psalm 51:10,17; Psalm 86:11; Proverbs 17:22;
Colossians 3:1.

WEEK 37: GOD THE GIVER

WEEK 37: GOD THE GIVER

DAY 1

LISTEN TO THE WORD

For God so loved the world that he gave his one and only Son,
that whoever believes in him shall not perish but have eternal life.
(John 3:16)

This week we will continue to explore the truth that God is a giver. The most famous Scripture in the Bible tells us that God so loved that he GAVE.

It is God's very nature to give. And the most extravagant gift he ever gave was the gift of his one-of-a-kind Son. It was a gift of astonishing love. God saw a world that was rebelling against him, running from him, ignoring him — and he gave his perfect Son to that world. If we receive that gift — if we put our confidence in God's Son — we can trade our dying for his life. God is a giver, and he gives us the gift of his Son.

LIVE THE WORD

We are most like God when we give. Make arrangements right now to give a small gift to someone today as an expression of the love of our giving God.

DAY 2

LISTEN TO THE WORD

And he took bread, gave thanks and broke it, and gave it to them,
saying, "This is my body given for you; do this in remembrance of me."
(Luke 22:19)

Jesus, who perfectly discloses the heart of God the Father, is the most
generous giver who ever breathed the atmosphere of the earth. He gave
food to hungry stomachs. He gave sight to blind eyes. He gave purity
to leprous skin and motion to paralyzed limbs. He gave hope to hurting hearts. But he gave more. Every time we eat the Lord's Supper, we
remember that Jesus even gave his body for us. He presented his back to
endure our scourging. He offered his head to accept our crown of thorns.
He stretched out his hands to receive our nails. He went to our cross and
died our death. His body was given for us.

LIVE THE WORD

Picture in your mind Jesus on the cross, and meditate on that picture
for a moment. Imagine him speaking to you, saying, "This is my body,
given for you."

DAY 3

LISTEN TO THE WORD

And hope does not put us to shame, because God's love
has been poured out into our hearts through the Holy Spirit,
who has been given to us.
(Romans 5:5)

Our giving God even gives us himself — he gives us his Holy Spirit.

One of the most surprising claims of the Bible is that God longs to give his Holy Spirit to you. His Spirit wants to take up residence in your heart and have an interactive relationship with you. He wants to guide you and convict you and encourage you. He wants to fill you to overflowing with his presence.

We might expect God to keep his Holy Spirit a gazillion miles away from unholy folks like us, but he doesn't. He gives his Spirit to us.

LIVE THE WORD

Ask God to fill you with his Spirit. Tell him you don't want to settle for a small dose, but you want your life and your character to overflow with him.

DAY 4

LISTEN TO THE WORD

For the wages of sin is death, but the gift of God is
eternal life in Christ Jesus our Lord.
(Romans 6:23)

Death is deserved — it is the payment we have earned with our sin. But life is a gift from God through Jesus Christ. Our giving God offers us eternal life. To say that the life he gives is eternal obviously says something about the duration of that life. It is life that never ends. It doesn't cease with your last breath and your last heartbeat. It continues infinitely on the other side of the grave.

To say that the life God gives is eternal also says something about the quality of that life. It is God's kind of life. It is life that is no longer dead to the ultimate reality of the universe. It is the life you were created for — life with ultimate meaning and significance — life connected to God.

LIVE THE WORD

Thank God for the gift of life — both physical life and eternal life.

Week 37: God the Giver

Day 5

Listen to the Word

Every good and perfect gift is from above,
coming down from the Father of the heavenly lights,
who does not change like shifting shadows.
(James 1:17)

God is the source of every good thing we have. That includes the gifts listed in Scripture that we have explored for the last two weeks, such as strength, peace, wisdom, a new heart, and eternal life. But that also includes sunsets and chocolate milkshakes and your family and the money in your pocket and the oxygen you just inhaled. The only reason you have any of it is because he is generous and he loves to give. If it is good, it is from God.

Live the Word

Make a quick list of ten good gifts in your life. Thank God for all of them.

Week 38: Mouth Filter

DAY 1

LISTEN TO THE WORD

Do not let any unwholesome talk come out of your mouths,
but only what is helpful for building others up according to their needs,
that it may benefit those who listen.
(Ephesians 4:29)

Your words have tremendous power for good. They can give direction to the lost, or encouragement to the broken, or hope to the desperate. Your words can bring life. But your words can also kill. They can be weapons that wound a soul or ruin a reputation. They can spew verbal venom on everyone within earshot.

God has a plan for the way you use your mouth. We will spend the week reflecting on what he reveals of that plan in Ephesians 4:29. Many of us have such struggles with the way we use words that this single verse could give us plenty to work on for the next several years. May God use this verse to make your mouth his instrument.

LIVE THE WORD

Commit Ephesians 4:29 to memory, or write it on a card and keep that card in a prominent place this week.

DAY 2

LISTEN TO THE WORD

Do not let any unwholesome talk come out of your mouths,
but only what is helpful for building others up according to their needs,
that it may benefit those who listen.
(Ephesians 4:29)

"What you say is what you are." That expression from childhood rings true. Jesus put it this way: "Out of the overflow of the heart, the mouth speaks." In other words, the quality of your speech reveals the health of your heart. Ugly words flow from an ugly heart. Kind words flow from a kind heart.

This means that if you struggle with words, your challenge is bigger than you thought. You don't just have a language problem — that unwholesome talk is a sure-fire indicator that you have a heart problem. You need more than an improved vocabulary — you need a new heart.

LIVE THE WORD

Ask God to transform your heart. Ask him to shape it according to his compassion and purity, and ask him to cause your heart to produce words that honor him.

DAY 3

LISTEN TO THE WORD

Do not let any unwholesome talk come out of your mouths,
but only what is helpful for building others up according to their needs,
that it may benefit those who listen.
(Ephesians 4:29)

Our Scripture warns you that unwholesome talk will try to sneak out of your mouth. It is your job to prevent it from exiting. God calls you to set up a security checkpoint at your lips. He wants you to do a thorough examination of each word before it is said. If there are words that would wound, they don't get clearance to pass. If there are words that are dishonest, they have to stay behind. Anything that is unwholesome is unwelcome beyond the gate of your lips.

Much of your problem with words stems from the absence of this kind of security checkpoint. Any words that pop into your mind pop out of your mouth. Instead of practicing that kind of unfiltered communication, you must evaluate each word before you speak it. If the words you are considering don't honor God, then don't let them out of your mouth.

LIVE THE WORD

Be intentional about thinking before you speak today. When unwholesome words present themselves at your lips, choose to leave them unspoken.

DAY 4

LISTEN TO THE WORD

Do not let any unwholesome talk come out of your mouths,
but only what is helpful for building others up according to their needs,
that it may benefit those who listen.
(Ephesians 4:29)

According to Ephesians 4:29, the only words that we should allow to come out of our mouths are words that build others up and benefit those who listen.

Imagine how rare speech would be if we simply left unsaid all the things that didn't meet those criteria. Imagine a day without grumbling, bragging, exaggeration, reputation assassination, cruel humor, or pointless yammering. Imagine a day where all the negative words, and even the neutral words, are left out — and all that is left is encouraging, helpful communication. Imagine a day when the only words that are spoken are those that actually represent an improvement over silence!

LIVE THE WORD

Listen to the words you hear all around you today, and notice how few of them live up to the standards in Ephesians 4:29. Ask God to use this exercise to train you to use your words only in ways that honor Him.

DAY 5

LISTEN TO THE WORD

Do not let any unwholesome talk come out of your mouths,
but only what is helpful for building others up according to their needs,
that it may benefit those who listen.
(Ephesians 4:29)

We often use words to tear others down. We also speak for the purpose of building ourselves up, hoping that our words will make us appear to be intelligent or funny or important or charming. Our Scripture calls us instead to use words to build others up according to their needs.

Your words can make a positive difference in the lives of the people around you today. They can bring hope to someone who is hurting. They can speak a compliment to someone who hasn't heard one in weeks. They can express appreciation to someone who thought nobody noticed. They can reveal your love and God's love to someone who was convinced that nobody cared. Who will you build up today?

LIVE THE WORD

Ask God to help you speak encouraging words every time you open your mouth today. Ask him to give you opportunities to build others up according to their needs.

WEEK 39: DOUBT

DAY 1

LISTEN TO THE WORD

Immediately the boy's father exclaimed,
"I do believe; help me overcome my unbelief!"
(Mark 9:24)

This week we will reflect on the topic of doubt. Like the father in Mark 9, most of us are a mixture of faith and doubt. Sometimes your heart believes, but your mind is still catching up. Sometimes what once seemed like a solid foundation starts to feel like shaky ground. We like it when our statements of faith have a period at the end, or even an exclamation point, but sometimes there is a question mark hanging there.

Know that you are not alone in your doubt. The Bible is full of faith heroes who had questions about their faith — folks like Abraham and Sarah, Moses, Gideon, Mary, John the Baptist, Peter, and Thomas. They all learned that God can do impressive things with doubting faith.

LIVE THE WORD

If you are struggling with doubt, make the words of the father in Mark 9 your prayer this week: "I do believe; help me overcome my unbelief."

DAY 2

LISTEN TO THE WORD

For now we see only a reflection as in a mirror;
then we shall see face to face. Now I know in part;
then I shall know fully, even as I am fully known.
(1 Corinthians 13:12)

Doubt is not a sin. It is a sin to refuse to believe — but the doubter is trying to believe. It is a sin to be content in the dark — but the doubter is searching for light. It is a sin to be indifferent about God — but the doubter wants to know God, yet doesn't have him all figured out.

Doubt is normal. Our limited perspective does not allow us to take in the whole picture (we just see "a poor reflection"), so it is quite natural that questions would arise. Trying to comprehend God is like trying to fit the Pacific Ocean in a cup. Doubt is the natural result of using limited brain cells to grasp a limitless God.

LIVE THE WORD

Memorize 1 Corinthians 13:12. Ask God to call it to your mind in times when you don't have all the answers.

WEEK 39: DOUBT

DAY 3

LISTEN TO THE WORD

...Truly I tell you, if you have faith as small as a mustard seed,
you can say to this mountain, "Move from here to there" and it
will move. Nothing will be impossible for you.
(Matthew 17:20)

We often assume that if we want to see God at work, we have to
have really big faith. We fear that if we don't have 100%, bold, super-
committed, giant-sized belief, then we are out of luck. But Jesus says it is
not the size of your faith that matters, but the size of the object of your
faith. God can take faith as miniscule as a mustard seed and do impressive things with it. God can work with doubting faith.

Your faith may not be very strong, but your God is!

LIVE THE WORD

Thank God that his work in your life has much more to do with how
big he is than with how big your faith is.

DAY 4

LISTEN TO THE WORD

Then Jesus told him, "Because you have seen me, you have believed;
blessed are those who have not seen and yet have believed."
(John 20:29)

Thomas was one of the more famous doubters in the Bible. The risen Jesus obliterated his doubts by standing before him, nail prints and all. Then Jesus spoke the surprising words of John 20:29. He said that doubting folks like us are the really fortunate ones — folks who have the opportunity to believe without seeing, to trust without having all our questions wiped away.

Trusting God when you have all the answers is not faith — it is common sense. When you don't understand fully, then you have the opportunity to trust fully. Striving to trust God through your doubt produces a faith that is more fully alive. It produces a faith that is really yours, and not just an unexamined hand-me-down. God can use doubt to grow your faith. Blessed are those who have not seen and yet have believed.

LIVE THE WORD

Ask God to use your doubts to bring you into a fuller, deeper faith.

Week 39: Doubt

Day 5

Listen to the Word

Is anything too hard for the LORD? (Genesis 18:14)

If you have a friend who doubts that a huge, heavy airplane could actually get airborne, it wouldn't do much good to tell them to try harder to believe. The best plan would be to take them to an airport where they could watch planes take off. Likewise, trying harder to believe in God is unproductive. But the more you watch God and get to know him, the more natural it becomes to have confidence in him.

God told Abraham and Sarah that they were going to have a baby, in spite of the fact that they were infertile and their combined age was 190. Their doubtful response was to laugh their heads off. God then asked the great question recorded in Genesis 18:14: "Is anything too hard for the Lord?" He answered that question with a loud "no" by sending Isaac nine months later. The more we watch God, the easier it becomes to believe that nothing is too hard for him.

Live the Word

Write the question from Genesis 18:14 on a card and put it somewhere you will see it for the next couple of weeks.

Week 40: Perseverance

DAY 1

LISTEN TO THE WORD

…Let us throw off everything that hinders and the sin that so easily entangles. And let us run with perseverance the race marked out for us. (Hebrews 12:1)

The Bible says you are a runner. You may not consider yourself a runner. You may even think runners are missing some important mental hardware. Perhaps you wouldn't even run if you were being chased by a hungry grizzly bear. But the Bible says you are a runner. Your life is a long distance race that must be run with perseverance.

This week we will ponder the Bible's call to perseverance. God wants you to know that you can make it to the finish line. You can keep going even when things get hard. When you get knocked down, you can get back up and keep running. You can refuse to quit. You can persevere.

LIVE THE WORD

Ask God to give you perseverance. Commit to him that with his help, you will keep living for him through this week, even when it would be easier to give up.

DAY 2

LISTEN TO THE WORD

Consider it pure joy, my brothers and sisters,
whenever you face trials of many kinds, because you know
that the testing of your faith produces perseverance.
(James 1:2–3)

Speaking of "pure joy," sweet tea is one of my favorite delicacies. You have probably noticed that when you add sugar to tea, the sugar settles to the bottom. The only way to make the tea sweet is to stir it. It is the stirring that causes the sugar to permeate the entire pitcher of tea.

You are the pitcher of tea, and your faith is the sugar. That faith is in you, but it doesn't really transform you until there is some stirring. That stirring is what James refers to as "trials of many kinds." God uses the trials you experience to change you and make you stronger. When your life gets stirred up, God uses it to build your perseverance. In fact, it is impossible to develop perseverance without that kind of stirring. The only way to develop a "never give up" attitude is to survive something that tempts you to give up. God is so good that even your trials can be reason to rejoice, because those trials strengthen your perseverance.

LIVE THE WORD

Read Romans 8:18 and 2 Corinthians 4:17. Ask God to help you believe that the hard things we endure in life are nothing compared to the great things God has in store for us.

DAY 3

LISTEN TO THE WORD

Not only so, but we also glory in our sufferings,
because we know that suffering produces perseverance.
(Romans 5:3)

Like yesterday's verse, today's Scripture calls us to do something that sounds a little silly: rejoice when things are hard. If you are like me, joy is not your first response when a sinus infection strikes or a check bounces or a friend snubs you. But the Bible reminds us that God is so good, he can take the bad things you endure and turn them into the very good thing of perseverance. God uses suffering to build your spiritual muscles. He takes problems that may have been meant to destroy you, and he uses them to strengthen you. God can use your pain for his glory and for your good.

LIVE THE WORD

What is your most difficult struggle today? Ask God to help you endure it, and ask him to help you find a measure of joy in the way he can use that trial to develop your perseverance.

DAY 4

LISTEN TO THE WORD

I have fought the good fight, I have finished the race,
I have kept the faith.
(2 Timothy 4:7)

Paul provides us with a powerful example of perseverance. He survived beatings, floggings, imprisonment, stoning, shipwrecks, physical illness, deprivation, rejection, and just about every other difficulty you could imagine. But he never gave up. He kept serving God. And at the end of his life, he could honestly look back and say, "I have finished the race."

I think Paul would say to you today, "Never give up. Finish the race. No matter how difficult things may be, keep running. You started strong, and then things got tough, but now is not the time to quit. God is faithful to strengthen you and sustain you, so lean into him and keep moving forward. Never give up!"

LIVE THE WORD

Write a brief prayer to God, asking him to help you finish what you have started for him.

DAY 5

LISTEN TO THE WORD

May the Lord direct your hearts into God's love
and Christ's perseverance.
(2 Thessalonians 3:5)

Today's Scripture says that God wants you to have more than just a small dose of perseverance. He wants you to have all of Christ's perseverance. And he wants to give it to you! He wants to give you the "never give up" spirit that allowed Jesus to fearlessly fulfill his mission — a mission he knew would lead to his execution. God wants to give you the perseverance that enabled Jesus to endure the cross, resisting the temptation to rescue himself from that unthinkable suffering. Jesus kept running the race. With God's help, you can, too.

LIVE THE WORD

Shape the words of today's Scripture into a prayer, and pray it continually today: "Direct my heart into your love and Christ's perseverance."

WEEK 41: ANXIETY

WEEK 41: ANXIETY

DAY 1

LISTEN TO THE WORD

Humble yourselves, therefore, under God's mighty hand,
that he may lift you up in due time. Cast all your anxiety on him
because he cares for you.
(1 Peter 5:6–7)

Do you struggle with stress? Are you worried and anxious? Is there something you are facing that makes you want to pull your hair and scream, or pull someone else's hair and scream? If so, this week's Scripture will offer you some hope.

Peter encourages you to cast all your anxiety on God. The Greek word that is translated "cast" literally means "throw upon." Just toss your concerns at God. Fling your worries away to him like you are bailing water out of a leaky boat. You don't have to carry your cares alone. God wants to help. Give all your stress to him!

LIVE THE WORD

The next time you notice yourself feeling worried today, let it be a cue to pray. Take the thing you are stressed about and cast it on God in prayer.

DAY 2

LISTEN TO THE WORD

Humble yourselves, therefore, under God's mighty hand, that he may
lift you up in due time. Cast all your anxiety on him
because he cares for you.
(1 Peter 5:6–7)

Peter's instruction for dealing with worry begins in an unexpected place — he challenges us to be humble. At first glance, that seems like advice with no connection to the problem of anxiety. But consider Peter's wisdom. How much of your stress comes from viewing yourself as the center of the universe? If you think you are the star and it is all about you, then the slightest ripple in your financial situation, or the smallest health concern, or the most insignificant personal insult will seem to be the end of the world. But if you are humble — if you live for God and others — those personal trials still hurt, but they are not so earthshaking.

And how much of your stress comes from trying to lift yourself up in the eyes of others? You probably spend significant energy managing your image, attempting to appear smart or spiritual or funny or pretty. That project always produces anxiety. But if you ignore your public approval ratings and trust God to lift you up, you have significantly less to be worried about.

LIVE THE WORD

Ask God to help you live for him. Tell him you want to stop worrying about how others perceive you.

DAY 3

LISTEN TO THE WORD

Humble yourselves, therefore, under God's mighty hand, that he may
lift you up in due time. Cast all your anxiety on him
because he cares for you.
(1 Peter 5:6–7)

Peter calls our attention to God's mighty hand. Trusting God's might
is a crucial step in letting go of your worry. If God is not mighty, then you
have reason to be nervous. If God is watching you wrestle with life and
helplessly wringing his hands, wishing he could do something for you,
then you might as well stock up on the antacids and learn to live with the
migraines. But if God is mighty enough to ignite the sun, do you think
there might be an outside chance he's strong enough to light your path?
God is big enough to handle the things you are worried about.

LIVE THE WORD

Take a moment to do an honest evaluation of your situation. Compare
the strength of the things you are struggling with to the strength of God.
Ask God to give you confidence in his might.

DAY 4

LISTEN TO THE WORD

Humble yourselves, therefore, under God's mighty hand, that he may
lift you up in due time. Cast all your anxiety on him
because he cares for you.
(1 Peter 5:6–7)

Peter says the most important antidote to anxiety is the simple fact
that God cares for you. If God doesn't care, then you have reason to be
anxious. If God sees the bad things that happen in your life and says, "Big
deal, I've got six billion more, and I can always make another," then get
used to the stress. But if God cares enough for birds to make sure they are
well fed, is it at least remotely possible he will take care of you? You don't
have to worry, because your Creator is watching out for you. You don't
have to be full of cares, because God cares for you.

LIVE THE WORD

Thank God for caring for you, and ask him to remind you of his
compassion the next time you begin to feel anxious.

WEEK 41: ANXIETY

DAY 5

LISTEN TO THE WORD

Humble yourselves, therefore, under God's mighty hand, that he may
lift you up in due time. Cast all your anxiety on him
because he cares for you.
(1 Peter 5:6–7)

One key to releasing anxiety is to trust God's timing. Peter promises that God will lift you up "in due time." God does not always come
through as quickly as we would like. We would prefer to have instant
relief from all of our troubles, and sometimes he lets those troubles linger
so that he can use them to grow us and shape us. We sometimes wish he
would hurry, but his timing is always perfect. If you know that God's
hand is mighty, and you know that he cares for you, and you know that
he is always right on time, then you have no reason to be overcome with
anxiety.

LIVE THE WORD

Cast your biggest source of stress on God in prayer, and ask him to
handle it in his perfect timing.

Week 42: Incomparable Christ

WEEK 42: INCOMPARABLE CHRIST

DAY 1

LISTEN TO THE WORD

The Son is the image of the invisible God. (Colossians 1:15)

In Colossians 1:15–20, Paul begins thinking about how amazing Jesus is, and he can't stop piling on the praise. This week we will examine some of the phrases he uses there to describe the incomparable Christ.

Paul says that Jesus is the exact, visible representation of the invisible God. When you look at Jesus, you see the God who can't be seen. He is the best picture of God ever taken. He illuminates God's essence. Paul reiterates the point in verse 19, telling us that all of God's fullness dwells in Christ. Jesus is God in the flesh. He has the same character, the same compassion, and the same courage. If you want to know what God is like, look at Jesus. He is the image of the invisible God.

LIVE THE WORD

Ask God to help you see him more clearly this week as you take a fresh look at Jesus, who is the perfect picture of his Father.

Day 2

Listen to the Word

For in him all things were created: things in heaven and on earth, visible and invisible, whether thrones or powers or rulers or authorities; all things have been created through him and for him.
(Colossians 1:16)

Colossians 1 informs us that the incomparable Christ is the architect and builder of the entire cosmos. It says "all things" were created in and through him. Presumably that includes three-toed sloths and walruses. "All things" includes the constellation Orion and chocolate pie. It includes the people you love. It includes love itself — he created that, too.

Not only was everything created in and through him, but everything was created "for him." He is the reason that what is, is. Everything in the universe finds its purpose in Jesus. The world was made by his power and for his pleasure. All things were created in, through, and for him.

Live the Word

Ponder the truth that you were created for Jesus. What does that mean? How should that affect the way you live?

WEEK 42: INCOMPARABLE CHRIST

DAY 3

LISTEN TO THE WORD

He is before all things…. (Colossians 1:17)

Kids at preschool love to be the line leader. It is a big privilege to be first. As Paul goes on bragging on the incomparable Christ in Colossians 1, he tells us that Jesus is the ultimate line leader. He is first of all.

Jesus is before everything else in time. Though he had a birthday a little over 2000 years ago, that day was not the beginning of his existence. Jesus has always been. He is before all things. He was before the beginning.

Jesus is also before everything else in priority. Above all the other important things in life, Jesus is ultimate. He comes first. He is before all things.

LIVE THE WORD

There is probably something in your life that is pushing to come before Jesus today. Ask Christ to help you put it in its proper place: after him.

DAY 4

LISTEN TO THE WORD

...In him all things hold together. (Colossians 1:17)

As Paul admires the incomparable Christ in Colossians 1, he gives Jesus praise for the fact that the universe is running. Our cosmos is not a self-sufficient system. It is because of Christ that gravity works, and the earth revolves around the sun, and day follows night. He's got the whole world in his hands! Jesus is the superintendent of the solar system, the divine glue that keeps everything in place. It would all fall apart without him. In him all things hold together.

LIVE THE WORD

What is your biggest source of stress today? Give it to Christ in prayer. Trust that the one who holds the universe together can hold you together today.

WEEK 42: INCOMPARABLE CHRIST

DAY 5

LISTEN TO THE WORD

For God was pleased to have all his fullness dwell in him, and through him to reconcile to himself all things, whether things on earth or things in heaven, by making peace through his blood, shed on the cross.
(Colossians 1:19–20)

Colossians 1:15–20 makes it clear that Jesus is supreme. No matter how highly you think of him, you underestimate him. Paul concludes his praise of the incomparable Christ with a reminder that Jesus died to reconcile you and all of creation to God. Your relationship to God has been broken by your own tendency to defy him and ignore him. You are powerless to fix that problem on your own. But Christ repairs the relationship by dying in your place, paying your penalty. Jesus reconciles you to God.

LIVE THE WORD

Say a prayer of thanks to Christ. Praise him for dying to make you right with God.

WEEK 43: SERVANTHOOD

WEEK 43: SERVANTHOOD

DAY 1

LISTEN TO THE WORD

Sitting down, Jesus called the Twelve and said, "Anyone who wants to be first must be the very last, and the servant of all."
(Mark 9:35)

The world says: "To be great, you must be first. The greatest person is the one with the most toys, or the best grades, or the nicest hair, or the biggest house. If you want to be great, you must demonstrate that you are above others."

Jesus says: "To be great, you must be last. The greatest person is the one with the willing hand, and the listening ear, and the small ego. If you want to be great, you must put others above yourself."

Christ calls us to stop worrying about our own status and start paying attention to the needs of others. He calls us to view the people around us with eyes of compassion, not eyes of competition. He calls us to arrive at greatness by the path of servanthood.

LIVE THE WORD

Ask Jesus to help you believe that his path to greatness is the right one. Ask him to work in you this week to develop the heart of a servant in you.

DAY 2

LISTEN TO THE WORD

For even the Son of Man did not come to be served, but to serve,
and to give his life as a ransom for many.
(Mark 10:45)

Jesus not only calls us to serve — he shows us how. He blazes the trail for us. God's Son came to serve. When the High and Exalted One arrived on earth, he did not act high and exalted. He washed the smelly feet of his friends. He touched lepers. He spent time with children. He listened to losers and outcasts. He provided meals for hungry crowds. He prayed for people who despised him. Then as the definitive act of service for all time, he gave his life so you could be free.

If you want to know what a real servant looks like, look to Jesus. He traveled the path of servanthood. And he is calling you to follow him.

LIVE THE WORD

Be a servant to the next person you encounter. Don't be obnoxious about it or announce that you are serving them; simply treat them with the compassion of Christ and seek to put their needs above your own.

WEEK 43: SERVANTHOOD

DAY 3

LISTEN TO THE WORD

You, my brothers and sisters, were called to be free. But do not use your freedom to indulge the flesh; rather, serve one another humbly in love.
(Galatians 5:13)

God has given you an amazing gift: he has made you free. To a large extent, you are free to determine what you will do with the day before you. If you wish, you can use it to "indulge the sinful nature." You can spend the day obsessed with your own selfish wants, worries, plans, and pleasures. In Galatians 5:13, God calls you to a different use of your freedom. He challenges you to make the radical, free choice to spend this day making a difference in the lives of others. He calls you to serve others in love. How will you use your freedom today?

LIVE THE WORD

To listen to someone is a profound act of service. Today, slow down and really listen to the people who speak to you.

DAY 4

LISTEN TO THE WORD

Whoever serves me must follow me; and where I am,
my servant also will be. My Father will honor the one who serves me.
(John 12:26)

One of the main reasons we find serving to be such a struggle is that servants don't typically grab a lot of headlines. We want to be honored. We want to be thought of as "somebody." And let's face it — our world is more impressed with someone who can throw a 95-mile-per-hour fastball than with someone who can skillfully wield a mop. A royal scepter in the hand generally grabs more attention than a toilet brush. Serving does not appear to be the best path to acclaim and honor.

But appearances are wrong! Jesus says, "My Father will honor the one who serves me." Honor does come to those who serve! Your neighbors may not be impressed when you live as a servant, but your God is. Serving gains you respect and recognition from the only source that really counts.

LIVE THE WORD

Ask God to break your bondage to the opinions of others. Ask him to help you stop living for human applause and start living to hear him say, "Well done, good and faithful servant."

Week 43: Servanthood

Day 5

Listen to the Word

In your relationships with one another, have the same mindset as Christ Jesus: Who being in very nature God, did not consider equality with God something to be used to his own advantage; rather he made himself nothing, taking the very nature of a servant.
(Philippians 2:5–7)

We shy away from serving because it sounds so menial, so far beneath us. But consider Jesus. He has all power, all wisdom, and all majesty. The whole universe exists because of him and for him. He is the unchallenged King of everything. He is in very nature God. Yet he made himself nothing, taking the very nature of a servant.

If you ever think that serving would be too far for you to stoop, think again. Christ was big enough to hang the rings around Saturn, but not too big to grab a basin of water and a towel and wash his disciples' feet. If the matchless Messiah could become a servant, it won't be too much of a stretch for you.

Live the Word

Spend a moment giving praise to Jesus, our Servant Savior. Thank him for serving you, and ask him to teach you how to serve others.

Week 44: Thought Life

DAY 1

LISTEN TO THE WORD

Finally, brothers and sisters, whatever is true, whatever is noble, whatever is right, whatever is pure, whatever is lovely, whatever is admirable — if anything is excellent or praiseworthy — think about such things. (Philippians 4:8)

We will spend this week reflecting on the truth revealed in Philippians 4:8: the God who formed your mind cares about what you put in it. He cares about it because he knows that what you regularly bring before your mind eventually shapes your mind and determines the kind of person you become. Nothing "passes through" your mind — every book you read, every TV show you watch, every website you visit, every conversation you have will rewire your brain and shape you in significant ways. We think we can violate this principle. We might say, "That show I watch is a little trashy, but I don't let it affect me." That's like saying, "I'm going to step off the roof, but I will choose not to hit the ground." What you allow to occupy your cranial cavity will determine your speech, your actions, your decisions, and your destiny. What you think is what you are.

LIVE THE WORD

Keep track of where you mind goes today. How often is it filled with things that match the list in Philippians 4:8? How often is it focused on more harmful things?

DAY 2

LISTEN TO THE WORD

Finally, brothers and sisters, whatever is true, whatever is noble,
whatever is right, whatever is pure, whatever is lovely, whatever is
admirable — if anything is excellent or praiseworthy — think about
such things. (Philippians 4:8)

What you put in your gas tank has consequences for your car. NASCAR drivers don't settle for the cheapest fuel they can find. What you put in your mouth has consequences for your body. Eating two pounds of chocolate a day wouldn't exactly enhance your performance! Likewise, what you put in your mind has consequences for your character. If your mental diet consists primarily of movies with gutter language, video games full of gruesome violence, books and magazines based on lust, and conversations focused on gossip, then don't be surprised when your character is not so pretty.

Your thought life shapes you. If you fill your mind with junk, your character naturally starts to take the shape of the garbage you are consuming. But if you fill your mind with "whatever is true...noble...right... pure...lovely...admirable...excellent or praiseworthy," your character naturally takes on those qualities.

LIVE THE WORD

Spend a moment evaluating your typical entertainment choices. Consider setting some new personal policies to protect your mind.

WEEK 44: THOUGHT LIFE

DAY 3

LISTEN TO THE WORD

Finally, brothers and sisters, whatever is true, whatever is noble, whatever is right, whatever is pure, whatever is lovely, whatever is admirable — if anything is excellent or praiseworthy — think about such things. (Philippians 4:8)

We are shaped by what we think about, so it is wise to fill our minds with good things. It may be so obvious it is not worth saying, but the best thing with which we can fill our minds is God. One key step toward having a healthy mind that honors God is to spend time thinking about him. Ponder how God has revealed himself in Scripture, in the world he has made, and in your life. Choose to dwell on him. Contemplate who he is — limitless, loving, loyal, perfect, and pure. He is excellent and praiseworthy! The more you invite him into your mind, the more he will be able to reshape it and renew it. As he renews your mind, he will transform you (Romans 12:2), molding you into the person he created you to be.

LIVE THE WORD

As you go through your routine today, try to think about God as frequently as you can. Notice how long you go without thinking of him. Make a game of it, trying to call him to mind as often as possible.

DAY 4

LISTEN TO THE WORD

Finally, brothers and sisters, whatever is true, whatever is noble, whatever is right, whatever is pure, whatever is lovely, whatever is admirable — if anything is excellent or praiseworthy — think about such things. (Philippians 4:8)

One great way to live out the instruction of Philippians 4:8 is to fill your mind with God's Word. You can take key portions of Scripture and make them permanent fixtures of your thought life.

You can meditate on a passage of Scripture: continually recall it to your mind, soak in its meaning, engage your imagination, and explore its connections with different facets of your life. You can memorize Scripture. Sometimes I make excuses that I am not good at memorizing, but then I realize that I can still sing every word of most of the songs I listened to in high school, and I can recite truckloads of useless sports trivia — I obviously have the ability to memorize things that matter to me. So do you. And the God who designed your brain will help you!

LIVE THE WORD

Meditate on this phrase from Philippians 4:9: "The God of peace will be with you." Reflect on those words throughout the day.

DAY 5

LISTEN TO THE WORD

Finally, brothers and sisters, whatever is true, whatever is noble,
whatever is right, whatever is pure, whatever is lovely, whatever is
admirable — if anything is excellent or praiseworthy — think about
such things. (Philippians 4:8)

God calls you to fill your mind with good things, because what fills
your mind will shape your character. All day long you are surrounded by
simple opportunities to obey his instruction. You can ponder a sunset or
a flower. You can savor a well-cooked meal. You can relish a good work
of literature or a moving piece of music. You can pay attention to little
acts of love and goodness that take place around you. You can learn something new; after all, all truth is God's truth, so even algebra class or The
Discovery Channel can give you the opportunity to live out Philippians
4:8. Reduce your intake of mental poison, and fill your mind with what
is true, noble, right, pure, lovely, admirable, excellent, and praiseworthy.

LIVE THE WORD

Commit Philippians 4:8 to memory.

WEEK 45: PEACE

WEEK 45: PEACE

DAY 1

LISTEN TO THE WORD

Peace I leave with you; my peace I give you. I do not give to you as the world gives. Do not let your hearts be troubled and do not be afraid.
(John 14:27)

We need peace. The daily headlines scream of this need. We look out at our world, and we see wars, terrorism, crime, and political battles. But the problem is not just "out there." We look inside at our hearts, and we see anxiety, hurry, and conflict. If someone could perform a spiritual MRI on you, they would probably find evidence of a stressed-out soul that is tied up in knots.

Get ready for some good news! For the next two weeks, we will explore two different verses in the Gospel of John in which Jesus promises to give us peace. We will turn to him for what we need.

LIVE THE WORD

Pray the following breath prayer as often as it comes to mind today and in the days ahead: "Jesus, I receive your peace."

DAY 2

LISTEN TO THE WORD

Peace I leave with you; my peace I give you. I do not give to you as the world gives. Do not let your hearts be troubled and do not be afraid.
(John 14:27)

Jesus makes it clear that peace is a state of the heart. He contrasts the condition of peace with the condition of a troubled heart. Jesus wants you to know that even when your circumstances are in chaos, your heart can be at peace.

Jesus wants to give you a peace that is real even when the house is a wreck and company is on the way and the kids are screaming and the phone is ringing and the grass is too high and the bank balance is too low and the dog is chewing on every three-dimensional object in the house. Jesus wants to give you peace that endures even when somebody you care about is angry with you. He wants to give you peace that survives even when unthinkable tragedy strikes from out of the blue. His peace is an inner strength that prevails in spite of the outer circumstances.

LIVE THE WORD

How would you fill in the blank in this statement: I have trouble staying calm and peaceful when _____. Whatever goes in that blank, give it to Christ, and ask him to help you be at peace in him even in those circumstances.

DAY 3

LISTEN TO THE WORD

Peace I leave with you; my peace I give you. I do not give to you as the world gives. Do not let your hearts be troubled and do not be afraid. (John 14:27)

Jesus makes it clear that the enemy of peace is fear. As he offers us his peace, he tells us not to be afraid.

Peace and fear are like two different sets of glasses through which we look at the future. With fear glasses, we look ahead and see all the bad things that might happen: heartache, pain, and all sorts of gloom and doom. With peace glasses, we look ahead and recognize that Christ holds us no matter what comes. When we remember we are in his hands, fear becomes absolutely unnecessary, and we are filled instead with peace.

LIVE THE WORD

What are you afraid of today? Ask Jesus to replace your fear with his peace.

DAY 4

LISTEN TO THE WORD

Peace I leave with you; my peace I give you. I do not give to you as the world gives. Do not let your hearts be troubled and do not be afraid.
(John 14:27)

Jesus makes an obvious point in this week's verse that we could easily forget: peace is a gift. It is not something we achieve — it is something we receive. We don't attain it through strenuous effort or impressive intellect or super spirituality. We accept it as a free gift from Jesus. He gives it to those who walk with him. It is part of the fruit of the Spirit — a natural consequence of a life connected to him. We don't engineer our own peace — we let Jesus give us his.

LIVE THE WORD

Thank God for being the giver of every good and perfect gift. Acknowledge to him that you could never deserve what he graciously gives.

DAY 5

LISTEN TO THE WORD

Peace I leave with you; my peace I give you. I do not give to you as the world gives. Do not let your hearts be troubled and do not be afraid.
(John 14:27)

Jesus doesn't just say he gives us any old peace — he promises to give us HIS peace. Wow! He wants to give us the same peace he has, and that is a lot of peace. He is, after all, the Prince of Peace. He wants us to have the same peace that allowed him to sleep soundly on a boat in the midst of a storm. He wants us to have the same peace that allowed him to speak the very words of this week's verse while he could hear boots hitting the path — the boots of the soldiers coming to arrest Him. He wants us to have the same peace that was with him during his brutal crucifixion, allowing him to pray for those who were causing his pain. Christ wants you to have his peace.

LIVE THE WORD

Be bold enough to ask Jesus for what he promises to give — not just a little peace, but the full-size, unconquerable peace that is found in him.

WEEK 46: PEACE

WEEK 46: PEACE

DAY 1

LISTEN TO THE WORD

I have told you these things, so that in me you may have peace. In this world you will have trouble. But take heart! I have overcome the world! (John 16:33)

This week we will continue to seek the peace Jesus promises to give. But notice that in this week's verse, peace is actually one of two things Jesus guarantees that we will have. He says we will have peace. That's great news! But he also says we will have trouble. "In this world you will have trouble."

Jesus does not say, "In me you may have peace, and you will never have another problem again — no sickness, no bad weather, no traffic tickets, no acne or hair loss." Jesus honestly informs you that you will have trouble. You can count on it. It is part of being human. But just as trouble is a consistent side effect of life in a fallen world, peace is an automatic result of being connected to the One who has overcome the world. In him you may have peace!

LIVE THE WORD

Ask Jesus to help you stay in step with him today so that you can enjoy the benefit of his peace.

DAY 2

LISTEN TO THE WORD

I have told you these things, so that in me you may have peace. In this world you will have trouble. But take heart! I have overcome the world!
(John 16:33)

We hear Jesus promise to give us peace, and we think, "Alright! No more conflict, no more hard stuff, no more worries. Life is going to be a relaxing vacation on a Caribbean island from now on!" But before we even get our swimsuits packed, Jesus says, "In this world, you will have trouble."

We assume that peace and trouble are two opposite things. Either we have trouble, or we have peace. Peace, we presume, is the absence of trouble — it is life without deadlines, bills, arguments, and pop quizzes. But Jesus promises a peace that is more than the absence of trouble. He gives a peace that is stronger than trouble — a peace that sustains us even when troubles come.

LIVE THE WORD

Reflect on a time in your past when the peace of Christ sustained you even in difficult circumstances. Ask him to give you that same peace in the middle of today's troubles.

DAY 3

LISTEN TO THE WORD

I have told you these things, so that in me you may have peace. In this world you will have trouble. But take heart! I have overcome the world!
(John 16:33)

Jesus is up front about the fact that you will have trouble. But he says that in him, you can have peace anyway. In him, you can have a soul that is peaceful even when your circumstances are not. His peace is portable — you can carry it with you into any situation. And his peace is indestructible — nothing that happens to you has the power to take it away. Regardless of the condition of your surroundings, peace can be the condition of your soul. Even if your circumstances are going crazy, you can be calm in him.

LIVE THE WORD

Think of someone you know whose circumstances are difficult today. Pray that they will experience Christ's peace in the midst of their trouble.

DAY 4

LISTEN TO THE WORD

I have told you these things, so that in me you may have peace. In this world you will have trouble. But take heart! I have overcome the world!
(John 16:33)

How can you have peace when the world gives you so much trouble? Jesus answers that question by announcing that he has overcome the world. He says the world will come after you, but he has already conquered the world. The world is a defeated enemy. It is still fighting, but its fate is sealed.

Christ is working to give you peace. The world is working to take that peace away. And it is not a fair fight! Peace is possible, even in a world filled with trouble, because Christ has overcome the world.

LIVE THE WORD

Say a prayer of thanksgiving to Jesus, praising him for being stronger than all of the challenges that face you.

DAY 5

LISTEN TO THE WORD

I have told you these things, so that in me you may have peace. In this world you will have trouble. But take heart! I have overcome the world! (John 16:33)

Where do we get this peace that Jesus promises to give? It is obviously something that would be handy to have, so where do we find it? Jesus clearly identifies the location of that peace. It is in him. "IN ME you may have peace," Jesus says. If you are looking for peace anywhere else, apart from him, you are out of luck.

Do you want to have peace? Have HIM. It is a package deal. It is like the peanut butter inside a Reese's cup — just part of it. If you have Christ, you can have peace. Keep your eyes on him, listen to him, follow him, and then enjoy the blessed byproduct of his peace.

LIVE THE WORD

Confess to Jesus your tendency to look for peace in the wrong places. Ask him to help you count on him to provide it.

WEEK 47: HEAVEN

WEEK 47: HEAVEN

DAY 1

LISTEN TO THE WORD

My Father's house has many rooms; if that were not so, would I have told you that I am going there to prepare a place for you?
(John 14:2)

There is a place in heaven made just for you. Jesus is fixing it up for you right now. And in many ways, you were made just for that place. Your stay on this planet is a brief layover — your ultimate destination is heaven.

We will spend this week reflecting on some Scriptures that describe the future home of Jesus' followers. We will see that it is an astonishing place that is much more than the pastel hangout of chubby angels, fluffy clouds, and chamber music. It is more than an endless church service. It is a reality beyond your wildest imagination. And if you can get a glimpse of it this week, it might give you some encouragement to face the challenges that lie before you on your way there.

LIVE THE WORD

Ask God to clarify your vision of heaven this week, and to use that vision to give you courage and hope here and now.

DAY 2

LISTEN TO THE WORD

(God) will wipe every tear from their eyes. There will be
no more death or mourning or crying or pain,
for the old order of things has passed away.
(Revelation 21:4)

Heaven will be absent of all the things that cause suffering and pain. It will involve the total lack of sin and all the yuck caused by sin. Imagine no more fighting over who controls the West Bank, or who controls the TV remote. No more dictators, famine, pop quizzes, or losing seasons. Envision playgrounds in place of cemeteries. Imagine newspapers without crime reports or obituaries. Picture life with no more colds and no more cancer. No broken homes and no broken hearts.

Imagine a life of perfect joy — the universe set free from the damaging effects of sin. That is how the Bible describes heaven.

LIVE THE WORD

Pray that this world will more closely resemble heaven. Pray as Jesus taught: "Your will be done on earth as it is in heaven."

DAY 3

LISTEN TO THE WORD

To the one who is victorious, I will give the right to sit
with me on my throne, just as I was victorious
and sat down with my Father on his throne.
(Revelation 3:21)

Somehow we have come to imagine heaven as an eternal retirement village where everybody sits around on a cloud and plays the harp all day. No wonder some folks aren't too excited about going there! But that is not the image we find in Scripture. Revelation 3:21 describes heaven as a promotion — a reassignment to more significant, fulfilling work. In heaven, we will somehow join Christ on his throne — join him in his ruling work. We will have the privilege and responsibility of partnering with him in his creative activity throughout the universe. We will finally get to taste all the adventure and creativity and fruitfulness for which we were made.

LIVE THE WORD

Ask God to use the earthly work you are doing today to prepare you for the heavenly assignment he has for you.

DAY 4

LISTEN TO THE WORD

For we know that if the earthly tent we live in is destroyed,
we have a building from God, an eternal house in heaven,
not built by human hands.
(2 Corinthians 5:1)

The Bible says heaven is your home.

Home is where you are loved and accepted. It is where you fit. Where you are comfortable and secure. Where your needs are met and your burdens are released. If you ever feel like an oddball, like you don't fit, like things are not quite right, there is good news — you are not home yet. This life, as rich as it is, is nothing compared to what is waiting for you. Heaven is home.

LIVE THE WORD

Thank God for loving you enough to prepare a permanent home for you in heaven with him.

DAY 5

LISTEN TO THE WORD

However, as it is written: "No eye has seen, no ear has heard, no mind has conceived what God has prepared for those who love him."
(1 Corinthians 2:9, NIV '84)

Imagine trying to describe the world to an infant in the womb. It would be impossible. The unborn child simply lacks the experience and the capacity to understand what awaits her. God faces an even bigger challenge trying to help us understand heaven. It is literally better than we could ever imagine.

We have spent the week reflecting on several snapshots of heaven that God has provided in the Bible. But the most important thing about heaven is this: God is there. He is central, and he fills every crack and crevice of the place. What makes heaven infinitely better than just another Disney World is the fact that God dwells there in all his splendor. We will be with him, and that will be heavenly.

LIVE THE WORD

Ask God to help you see him more clearly today.

WEEK 48: GOD'S QUESTIONS

WEEK 48: GOD'S QUESTIONS

DAY 1

LISTEN TO THE WORD

But the LORD God called to the man, "Where are you?" (Genesis 3:9)

One of the surprising things about the Bible is the number of times we find a question on the lips of God. God is constantly asking questions of his people. Clearly, this is not because God needs information. It is not that he is in the dark and he needs us to enlighten him. God knows everything. He asks the questions for our benefit. He asks the questions hoping that they will cause a light to come on in our souls.

The first question we hear God asking is in Genesis 3. Adam and Eve have disobeyed God, and they are attempting to hide from him (like that's gonna work). God, who of course knows exactly where they are, calls out, "Where are you?"

What is your answer to that question from God? Not just your physical location — God is not concerned with your GPS coordinates. He is asking where you are with him. Are you hiding from him, or are you ready to walk with Him?

LIVE THE WORD

Repeat the breath prayer "Here I am, Lord" as often as possible today. Let God know that you are ready to hear his voice and do what he calls you to do all day long.

DAY 2

LISTEN TO THE WORD

The LORD said, "What have you done?" (Genesis 4:10)

Early in Genesis, God is full of questions for his disobedient children. He sounds like a prosecuting attorney conducting a cross-examination. He has several queries for the first murderer, Cain. He asks him why he is angry. He asks him where his brother is. Then, he asks the question in today's Scripture: "What have you done?"

God has the same question for you when you disobey him. And he doesn't ask because he wasn't paying attention and he needs you to clue him in. He knows exactly what you have done. And he knows you need to acknowledge it. You need to get it out in the open by confessing it to him. As soon as you stop the hiding, God can start the healing.

LIVE THE WORD

Is there a sin you need to confess? Be honest with God about what you have done.

WEEK 48: GOD'S QUESTIONS

DAY 3

LISTEN TO THE WORD

…And the word of the LORD came to him:
"What are you doing here, Elijah?"
(1 Kings 19:9)

In 1 Kings 19, Elijah is in the middle of high-tailing it out of town. He is running for his life, running away from his mission field, running away from his mission as a prophet. Not surprisingly, God tracks him down. He asks him a question — actually asks him the same questions twice within just a few verses: "What are you doing here?"

That is a good question for you to ponder. What are you doing where you are? What is your purpose there? Are you where God wants you to be? And are you doing what God wants you to do in that place?

LIVE THE WORD

Ask God to place you where he wants you to be, and to help you be who he wants you to be in that place.

DAY 4

LISTEN TO THE WORD

Where were you when I laid the earth's foundation?
Tell me, if you understand.
(Job 38:4)

Like most of us, Job had a lot of questions for God. He wanted to know why there was so much pain, and why God wasn't running the universe the way it ought to be run. God responded to Job with an avalanche of questions of his own, asking Job to consider which of them was more qualified to be God. Job got real quiet real quick.

So how about you? Where were you when God laid the earth's foundation? Unless you were there, aiding God in the assembly of the universe, perhaps you should hush and let him do his job. You can trust the One who has been here since before the beginning, who made it all by his wisdom and power and love.

LIVE THE WORD

Confess to God your tendency to try to play God and run your own life. Ask him to use what he has made to remind you how much bigger than you he is.

WEEK 48: GOD'S QUESTIONS

DAY 5

LISTEN TO THE WORD

"To whom will you compare me? Or who is my equal?"
says the Holy One.
(Isaiah 40:25)

Our final question from God is a profound one. Who is in God's category? Who is like God? Let's see...well...hmm...that's a pretty short list! God uses this question to remind us that absolutely nothing compares to him. Nothing even comes close to his holiness, his might, his brilliance, his beauty, or his mercy. No one else can create like he can, or sustain like he can, or protect like he can, or provoke like he can, or rescue like he can. There is no one like our God!

LIVE THE WORD

Take a moment to praise God for being absolutely one-of-a-kind.

WEEK 49: CONFESSION

WEEK 49: CONFESSION

DAY 1

LISTEN TO THE WORD

If we confess our sins, he is faithful and just and will forgive us
our sins and purify us from all unrighteousness.
(1 John 1:9)

Confession is not easy. No one enjoys saying, "I was wrong. I made a mistake. I blew it. I am guilty." But confession is an essential practice for the follower of Christ. God calls you to confess your sin to him. No hiding, no evading, no justifying and rationalizing — just be honest about the fact that you have missed the mark.

1 John 1:9 describes two amazing things that happen when you confess your sin to God. First, he forgives you. That means he changes the way he looks at you. He chooses not to hold your disobedience against you anymore. He wipes the slate clean. Second, he purifies you. He not only deletes the sin from his record book — he scrubs it out of your soul. He not only changes the way he looks at you — he actually changes you. He cleans up the mess that your sin has made in your heart. If you will confess, he promises to forgive and to purify.

LIVE THE WORD

Ask God to teach you the value of confession this week. Pray that you will have a powerful experience of his forgiveness and cleansing.

DAY 2

LISTEN TO THE WORD

If we claim we have not sinned, we make him out to be a liar
and his word is not in us.
(1 John 1:10)

1 John 1:9 challenges us to confess our sin. It says that act has two results: God will forgive us, and he will purify us. The very next verse describes the alternative to confession: claiming we have not sinned. If we refuse to acknowledge our imperfection, we are pretending that we are perfect. In other words, the opposite of confession is hypocrisy. That act also has two results. First, we make God out to be a liar. God says we are flawed, but we say we know better than God. Second, God's word has no place in our lives. When we foolishly act as if we are faultless, we cut ourselves off from the blessings that come with a healthy relationship with God. Our hypocrisy shuts off the valve through which his wisdom, joy, and power flow to us. Confession may not be a pleasant experience, but it certainly beats the alternative.

LIVE THE WORD

Be honest with God about your tendency to try to hide your sin from him and from yourself. Ask him to help you bring it out into the open before him.

Day 3

Listen to the Word

I have swept away your offenses like a cloud, your sins
like the morning mist. Return to me, for I have redeemed you.
(Isaiah 44:22)

You can have the courage to confess your sin to God because he is a God of enormous mercy. He longs to forgive. He longs to sweep your mistakes away. He doesn't want you to admit your mistakes so he can wipe you out for them; he wants to wipe out your sins. They will be gone without a trace, like a morning fog that can't linger in the light and warmth of the sun.

Listen to God's pleas in today's Scripture — he is pleading with you to return to him. He has vanquished the sin that was keeping you from him, and he wants you to be with him.

His mercy is deeper and wider than you can imagine.

Live the Word

Thank God for completely forgiving the sins you have confessed to him. While you are at it, give him a few more things he can sweep away. Confess your sin, confident in his incomparable grace.

DAY 4

LISTEN TO THE WORD

Have mercy on me, O God, according to your unfailing love;
according to your great compassion blot out my transgressions.
(Psalm 51:1)

Perhaps the most famous prayer of confession recorded in the Bible is found in Psalm 51, in which David begs for God's cleansing after his adultery with Bathsheba. Notice the grounds on which David asks for forgiveness: "according to your unfailing love; according to your great compassion." David does not say, "according to the fact that what I did wasn't really that bad, forgive me" or "Let this one slide, because you know I really love you and I normally do the right thing, but there were extenuating circumstances this time, and..." David doesn't expect forgiveness because he deserves to receive it; he expects forgiveness because God delights to give it.

God does not forgive you because *you* are good. He forgives you because *he* is good. It is pure mercy, not merit. Cleansing is possible only because of the unfailing love and great compassion of God.

LIVE THE WORD

Ask God to help you examine yourself for things you need to confess to him — times you have done the wrong thing, or failed to do the right thing. Confess your sin to him, confident that forgiveness comes because of his mercy.

WEEK 49: CONFESSION

DAY 5

LISTEN TO THE WORD

But the tax collector stood at a distance. He would not
even look up to heaven, but beat his breast and said,
"God, have mercy on me, a sinner."
(Luke 18:13)

Jesus tells a story with an unexpected hero in Luke 18. He says two men go to the temple to pray. One has it all together. He is a Pharisee, well known for his devotion to God's law and traditional family values. He is devout and respectable. He stands and prays reciting his religious resume, reminding God how fortunate God is to have him on his team. The other man is a tax collector, a despised sell-out with no redeeming qualities. He hides in the corner, and the best he can do in prayer is to admit his depravity and beg for mercy. The punch line of the story is that the tax collector goes home in a right relationship with God, while the Pharisee departs no better than he was when the story began. Apparently, honest confession from sinful folks is God's kind of prayer.

LIVE THE WORD

Commit to make confession a regular part of your prayer experience, confident that God loves to show mercy. Ask God to help you to be consistent in honestly admitting your sin to Him.

WEEK 50: IMPACT

DAY 1

LISTEN TO THE WORD

Declare his glory among the nations,
his marvelous deeds among all peoples.
(Psalm 96:3)

This week's Scripture commands us to brag on God to the world. God wants you to tell everybody who he is and what he has done. You were made to be a missionary.

Something is wrong if you spend an hour every Sunday morning singing your heart out about how great God is, and about how proud of him you are, but then you leave the church and keep him to yourself for the rest of the week. You have a divine assignment to be a declarer. God wants you to be so impressed with him that you can't keep yourself from talking about him with anyone who will listen.

LIVE THE WORD

Tell God that you don't want your praise to be limited to Sundays, and you don't want it to be just between you and him. Ask him to help you to be willing to brag on him to others.

DAY 2

LISTEN TO THE WORD

Declare his glory among the nations,
his marvelous deeds among all peoples.
(Psalm 96:3)

Psalm 96:3 says it is your job to tell people how great God is. The verse commands you to declare two things. First, you are called to brag about God's "glory." That means declaring his essence, his majesty, his beauty, his God-ness.

Second, you are called to brag about his "marvelous deeds." That means announcing what he has done — calling attention to the fact that he is the one who designed the universe, the one who invented life and food and laughter and love. It means giving him public credit as the one who rescued you and the one who strengthens you to stand in hard times.

Tell people who God is and what he has done. Declare his glory and his marvelous deeds!

LIVE THE WORD

Think of one of the impressive things God has done in your life. Thank him for it, and ask him to give you an opportunity to tell someone else about it.

DAY 3

LISTEN TO THE WORD

Declare his glory among the nations,
his marvelous deeds among all peoples.
(Psalm 96:3)

Notice that it is our job to declare God's glory to all kinds of people in all kinds of places. The command in Psalm 96:3 obliterates any ethnic or geographic limitations we might place on our obligation. We can't get away with simply sharing with people we like, or people who are like us. God's love stretches to each person on the planet, and so does our responsibility.

Other well-known Scriptures point in the same direction. John 3:16 reminds us that God so loved the entire world. The Great Commission calls us to make disciples of all nations. Jesus' challenge in Acts 1:8 is to brag about him to the ends of the earth.

God wants everybody everywhere to know about him. And he wants us to tell them!

LIVE THE WORD

Intentionally reach across a relational boundary today. Be kind to someone who is different from you.

Day 4

Listen to the Word

Declare his glory among the nations,
his marvelous deeds among all peoples.
(Psalm 96:3)

Take a moment to think about some of the folks you encounter on a regular basis who are part of the "all peoples" of Psalm 96:3. What if they don't cross your path by accident? What if God sends them your way so that you can fill them in on what an amazing God he is? How can you brag on God to the people you will encounter today?

Could you start a new custom with your family of praying a prayer of thanksgiving at mealtime or bedtime? Could you tell the cashier at the grocery store about the ways God has used your church in your life and invite them to visit? Could you take advantage of an opportunity that arises with a neighbor to give God credit for your ability to survive some recent challenges? Could you tell a struggling friend that you will pray for them, and that you are confident that God is more than capable of meeting their needs? Simple actions like these are ways you can fulfill God's call to declare who he is and what he can do!

Live the Word

Add two or three more examples to the list above, and watch for opportunities that may present themselves during the day.

DAY 5

LISTEN TO THE WORD

Declare his glory among the nations,
his marvelous deeds among all peoples.
(Psalm 96:3)

When you obey the command in Psalm 96:3, it obviously benefits those who hear. People who have never known how great God is, or people who once knew but have forgotten, have a chance to hear about his glory and his marvelous deeds. Their lives can be changed by your words.

You also benefit when you obey the command. The more you declare his glory, the more clearly you see it. The more you point out his marvelous deeds, the more able to notice those deeds you become. Bragging on God leads to more passionately believing in God.

God gives you this command because others need to hear what you can tell them. He also gives the command because you need to do the telling. Declare his glory — for his sake, for their sake, and for your sake.

LIVE THE WORD

Reflect for a moment about the reasons you hesitate to tell others about him. Is it because you are afraid of their reaction? Is it because you aren't confident in your belief? Is it something else? Confess the source of your hesitation to God, and ask him to strengthen you.

WEEK 51: DOUBLE MINDED

WEEK 51: DOUBLE MINDED

DAY 1

LISTEN TO THE WORD

Come near to God and he will come near to you. Wash your hands,
you sinners, and purify your hearts, you double-minded.
(James 4:8)

James may have invented a word. Twice in his book he uses the Greek
word *dipsychos*, translated "double-minded." Historians have found no
recorded use of the word prior to the writing of the book of James. The
word literally means "double-souled" or "double-selfed."

How many of YOU are there? How many selves do you have? Do
your church friends know a different "you" that the people you hang
out with during the week wouldn't recognize? James warns us against the
tendency to be a different person in one set of circumstances than we are
in another — constantly bouncing back and forth from one set of values
and priorities to another.

This week we will hear God calling us to undivided, single-minded
devotion to him.

LIVE THE WORD

As you go through your day, pay attention to the ways you are
tempted to put on a different front for different groups of people. Ask
God to help you be one consistent person, consistently his.

WEEK 51: DOUBLE MINDED

DAY 2

LISTEN TO THE WORD

I am saying this for your own good, not to restrict you, but that you
may live in a right way in undivided devotion to the Lord.
(1 Corinthians 7:35)

Our Scripture calls us to live "in undivided devotion to the Lord."
We need to hear that challenge, because our devotion tends to be divided
among many different things. Maybe you would say, "What I want more
than anything is to be all yours, Lord. Well, being popular would be nice,
too. I'd like to be all yours, and be really well liked. And rich. You know,
Lord, just enough stuff so that I never have to worry about anything. So
all yours, and popular, and rich — that's what I want. And while you are
at it make sure I am healthy. And desirable. And influential. And…"

God desires and deserves to be the one you love more than anything.
He calls for undivided devotion.

LIVE THE WORD

What is God's primary competition for your loyalty right now —
what do you tend to want more than you want him? Confess that to him.

WEEK 51: DOUBLE MINDED

DAY 3

LISTEN TO THE WORD

I will give them singleness of heart and action,
so that they will always fear me and that all will go well for them
and for their children after them.
(Jeremiah 32:39)

Imagine two archers facing fifteen targets. One of the archers has a divided focus — he says, "I'm going to hit one of those targets. I'm not sure which one." He moves his bow back and forth and lets an arrow fly. Archer number two says, "I'm going to hit THAT one," and aims an arrow at a specific target. The second archer has what Jeremiah calls "singleness of heart and action," and his arrow is much more likely to hit the mark.

God says he can give us that kind of focus. He can give us the ability to cut through all of the competing concerns that clamor for our attention and help us zero in on him. He can align all that we desire and all that we do so that our whole lives are aimed right at the bullseye of knowing him and making him known.

LIVE THE WORD

Ask God to give you singleness of heart and action today. Ask him to help you to use everything on your to-do list as an opportunity to get to know him better and to help others to know him.

DAY 4

LISTEN TO THE WORD

With the tongue we praise our Lord and Father, and with it
we curse human beings, who have been made in God's likeness.
Out of the same mouth come praise and cursing.
My brothers and sisters, this should not be.
(James 3:9–10)

One of the clearest indicators of a heart that is not fully God's is
a mouth that is not fully God's. Our speech often gives evidence of
an inconsistent, divided life. Something is wrong when a mouth takes
frequent breaks from praise and prayer to spew gossip, insults, gutter
language, and other forms of verbal garbage.

If the faucet in your kitchen sink sometimes poured fresh water and
other times dispensed toxic sludge, you would be sure there was some
kind of significant problem. Likewise, if you hear your mouth bounce
back and forth between bragging on God and tearing down God's mas-
terpieces, you can be certain that God is still not finished making you all
his.

LIVE THE WORD

Pay extra attention to your words today. When you feel tempted to
speak destructive words, ask God to change your speech, and ask him to
change your heart.

WEEK 51: DOUBLE MINDED

DAY 5

LISTEN TO THE WORD

Teach me your way, Lord, that I may rely on your faithfulness;
give me an undivided heart, that I may fear your name.
(Psalm 86:11)

When you join the psalmist in asking God to give you an undivided heart, you are acknowledging that, currently, your heart is divided — you have a slice committed to this, a slice committed to that, and a slice committed to another thing. There is a civil war in your will. You have set your heart on too many things. Some of those things are evil and wrong, others are just less than the best, and all of them are in conflict with some of the others. Your heart is not fully his.

In praying this prayer, you also admit that the cure for your problem is beyond your own power. You can't put your heart back together. You need intervention from the divine heart surgeon. You need him to unite your heart so that the whole thing is devoted to him, and so that your relationship with him becomes the defining reality of your life instead of just another hobby. You need him to help you become all his.

LIVE THE WORD

As often as possible today, make the words of Psalm 86:11 your prayer.

WEEK 52: TODAY

WEEK 52: TODAY

DAY 1

LISTEN TO THE WORD

But if serving the LORD seems undesirable to you,
then choose for yourselves this day whom you will serve,
whether the gods your forefathers served beyond the Euphrates,
or the gods of the Amorites, in whose land you are living.
But as for me and my household, we will serve the LORD.
(Joshua 24:15)

Did you know that there is one day that is more important than all others in your relationship with God? Did you realize that there is a day that God has circled on his calendar as the day that is crucial in your growth as his child? That day is today. The Bible is full of verses that emphasize the critical importance of THIS DAY. We will explore some of those this week.

Joshua won't let us get by with an intention to SOMEDAY choose to serve God. He challenges us to make our choice THIS DAY. No procrastination. No excuses. No waiting for additional data to come in. Choose to serve God today.

LIVE THE WORD

Have you been waiting for the right time to give your life to God, or to serve him in some specific area? The right time is today. Tell God that you are choosing this day to go his way.

DAY 2

LISTEN TO THE WORD

This is the day the LORD has made; let us rejoice and be glad in it.
(Psalm 118:24, NIV '84)

We often relate rejoicing to days in the past — the day you got the game-winning hit, the day you made an A on that test, or the day she said "yes." Other times we think rejoicing is something we will do in the future — when you get that hoped-for raise, or make that long-awaited trip to the beach. We tend to endure today, suffering through it while remembering joyful yesterdays and anticipating joyful tomorrows.

God calls you to rejoice in THIS DAY. Today is God's day. He made it, and he gave it to you as a gift. He wants you to celebrate this day with him.

LIVE THE WORD

Think of some good things God has done for you this day, and tell him thanks for them. Smile while you tell him!

WEEK 52: TODAY

DAY 3

LISTEN TO THE WORD

Yet give attention to your servant's prayer and his plea for mercy,
LORD my God. Hear the cry and the prayer that your
servant is praying in your presence this day.
(1 Kings 8:28)

Solomon, who prayed the prayer recorded in today's Scripture, knew that the best day to pray is THIS DAY. We have good intentions to pray someday. One of these days, we hope to be prayer warriors, enjoying the fruit of a thriving prayer life. But we are a little busy today. We know prayer is important, but it doesn't seem quite as urgent as the other items screaming at us from our to-do lists. So we wait just one more day. And someday never comes.

The only way to live a life of prayer is to live days of prayer. You must pray today.

LIVE THE WORD

Stop what you are doing and pray — right now. Spend at least the next five minutes asking God for his help with the challenges you face today.

DAY 4

LISTEN TO THE WORD

...Today, if you hear his voice, do not harden your hearts
as you did in the rebellion.
(Hebrews 3:15)

Our Scripture reminds us of a choice you can make today: you can choose to hear God's voice. It is up to you whether you will spend this 24-hour slice of your life tuned in to God, or whether you will coast through it completely oblivious to him. You can choose to pay careful attention today to what he might be saying in what you read in Scripture, what you hear from his Spirit within you, and what you experience in your circumstances. Or you can harden your heart today and ignore him.

God wants to speak to you this day. Are you willing to listen?

LIVE THE WORD

Pray the following breath prayer as often as it comes to mind today: "Speak, Lord. I'm listening."

Week 52: Today

Day 5

Listen to the Word

Acknowledge and take to heart this day that the LORD is God in
heaven above and on the earth below. There is no other.
(Deuteronomy 4:39)

God is the only God. He is the High King of heaven. He is Lord of
every square inch of the earth. He has no legitimate competition — there
is no one even remotely like him. He is the only overwhelming God of
everything.

These things are true of God every day. But the Scripture says you
need to acknowledge them and take them to heart THIS DAY. Every day
life bombards you with competing gods clamoring for your attention,
and every day you are force-fed the myth that you are god and it is all
about you. So every day you must intentionally remind yourself who is
indeed on the throne. The Lord is God, and there is no other!

Live the Word

Be alert today to times when things other than God start to claim
center stage in your life. Every time they do, remind yourself that only
God is God.

CPSIA information can be obtained
at www.ICGtesting.com
Printed in the USA
FSOW02n1457261116
27725FS